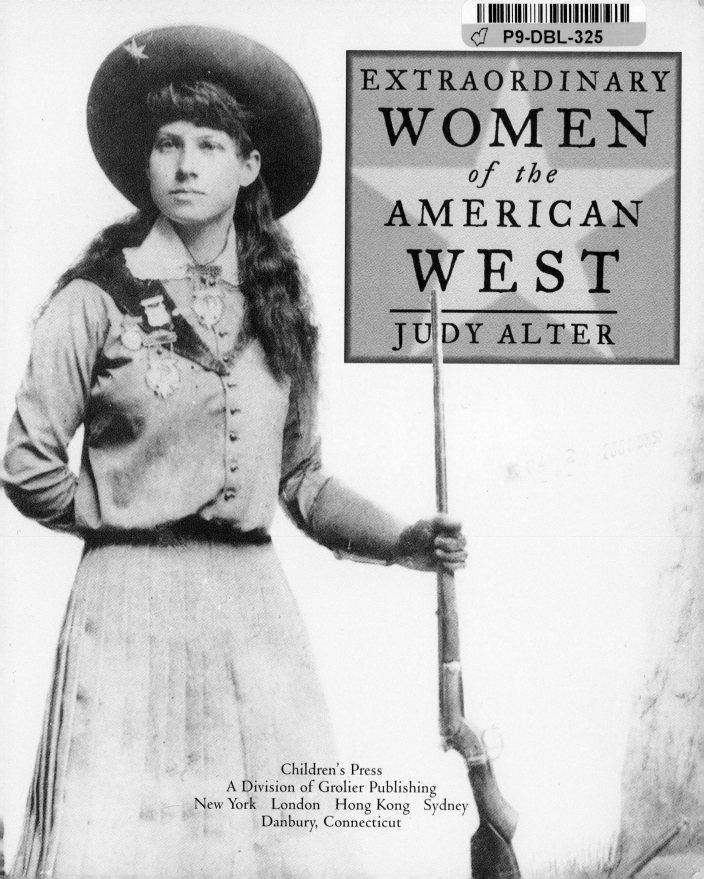

EXTRAORDINARY
WOMEN
of the
AMERICAN
WEST

JUDY ALTER

Children's Press
A Division of Grolier Publishing
New York London Hong Kong Sydney
Danbury, Connecticut

Library of Congress Cataloging-in-Publication Data
Alter, Judy

Extraordinary women of the American West / by Judy Alter.
p. cm. — (Extraordinary people)
Includes index.
Summary: Chronicles the exploits and achievements of more than fifty
women in the past and present of America's West, including the guide and
interpreter Sacajawea, journalist Jessie Benton Frémont, and author Willa Cather.

ISBN 0-516-20974-4 (lib. bdg.)   0-516-26465-6 (pbk.)
1. Women—West (U.S.)—Biography—Juvenile literature. 2. West (U.S.)—
Biography—Juvenile literature. [1. Women—West (U.S.)—   Biography. 2. West
(U.S.)—Biography.] I Title. II. Series.
CT3207.A58   1999
920.72'0978—dc21   98-5812

                                                                CIP
                                                                AC

Contents

46
Jessie Benton Frémont
1824–1902
Senator's Daughter,
Explorer's Wife

63
Molly Goodnight
1839–1926
Ranch Woman

79
Carry Nation
1846–1911
Reformer

51
Elisabet Ney
1833–1907
Sculptor

67
Sarah Winnemucca
1844?–1891
Champion of
Indian Rights

82
Mattie Castner
1848–1920
Hotelkeeper, "Mother
of Belt, Montana"

55
Mary Fields
1832–1914
Housekeeeper, Restaurateur,
Mail Carrier, and Laundress

70
Ann Eliza Webb Young
1844–1908?
Crusader Against
Polygamy

85
Pretty Shield
1850s?–1930s?
Crow Indian
Healing Woman

58
Abigail Scott Duniway
1834–1915
Women's Rights
Advocate

74
Nellie Cashman
1845–1925
Restaurant Owner
and Miner

88
Women on
the Stage

142

Miriam "Ma" Ferguson
1875–1961
Governor of Texas

158

Jessie Daniel Ames
1883–1972
Reformer

172

Lillian Riggs
1888–1977
Ranch Woman

146

Etta Place
1875?–1940s?
Outlaw's Partner

161

Edna Kahly Gladney
1886–1961
Pioneer of
Adoption Reform

176

Angie Debo
1890–1988
Author, Historian

149

Nancy Cooper Russell
1878–1940
Business Manager

165

Georgia O'Keeffe
1887–1986
Artist

180

Laura Gilpin
1891–1979
Photographer

153

Jeanette Rankin
1880–1973
Congresswoman
and Pacifist

169

**María Montoya
Martínez**
c. 1887–1980
Master Potter

184

Bessie Coleman
1893–1926
Pilot

234

Maria Tallchief
1925–
Ballerina

250

Patricia Schroeder
1940–
United States
Congresswoman

266

Ellen Ochoa
1958–
Astronaut

237

Sandra Day O'Connor
1930–
U. S. Supreme Court
Justice

254

Wilma Mankiller
1945–
Chief of the Cherokee
Nation of Oklahoma

268

**Charmayne
James-Rodman**
1970–
Barrel Racing
Champion

240

Ann Richards
1933–
Politician, Governor

259

Amy Tan
1952–
Novelist

271

Shannon Miller
1977–
Olympic Gymnast

245

Barbara Jordan
1936–1996
U. S. Representative,
Legislator, Teacher

261

Susan Butcher
1954–
Sled-dog racer

Who Settled the American West?

A frontier family poses in front of its sod house during the early 1890s.

Who settled the American West? According to legend, mountain men and trappers arrived first, followed by pioneers in covered wagons, cowboys, and soldiers—all men. The West, according to an old saying, was kind to men and dogs but tough on women and horses. It was a man's land.

But women were there. Most photographs show weary-looking women standing in front of dismal sod huts, with children clutching their ragged skirts. The expressions on their faces clearly show what they thought of life in the Old West. The settlers' wives in photographs are almost always white women. Not shown are the Native Americans who had always lived in the West, and the Hispanic settlers who had come there before white settlers arrived. Also missing are black pioneers, many of whom settled in Kansas and Oklahoma, and Chinese immigrants who formed small communities around mining towns. Often overlooked too are the many women who found excitement and joy in the West and led extraordinary lives.

The American Indian guide, Sacajawea, is among the first, if not the first, woman in the American West about whom there is a written record, though no doubt there were extraordinary women who had lived in the land for many years. What we know of women in the Old West is unbalanced because little was written and recorded about American Indian, black, and Hispanic women. Those who left the clearest trail in the 1800s are the Anglo (European white) women who came west from the East, often following their men. Many recorded their experiences in diaries, letters, articles, memoirs, and books.

The first white men who went west were the mountain men who began to explore in the 1830s and 1840s. They left their women behind. Early settlers in most parts of the West were also men without women. But in the mid-1840s, wagon trains began rolling across the Great Plains. The wagon trains carried families and brought such women as Narcissa Whitman to Oregon and Susan Magoffin to New Mexico. For women, the trip was probably almost unbearable. They rode in slow ox-drawn wagons so crammed with household goods that there was almost no place to sit. Some walked behind wagons and others walked behind ox-drawn carts. In the 1850s, a large number of Mormon women actually helped push handcarts from the Mississippi to Salt Lake City. Women carried children too young to walk and worried constantly over those old enough to wander into danger on the prairies.

Women's clothes were inappropriate for such a journey. Billowing full skirts either blew around their heads or dragged in the mud; hoopskirts and bustles were equally impractical. Women learned to wear high-topped shoes to protect their feet, bonnets that kept off the sun's burning rays, and long underwear for warmth in winter.

They had little privacy and no cosmetics. A good soaking bath was a rare luxury; more often, an outdoor stream was the tub—and Western river water tended to be the color of dirty soapsuds. A broken piece of looking glass or a piece of tin was their only mirror. Women used sour milk or buttermilk as a skin bleach, white wax or spermaceti—a salve made from whale oil—for their skin, and a light dusting of cornstarch for face powder.

But where did they go when they went "west"? Where does the American West begin? Are California and North Dakota—such different places—all part of the same American West? Generally, we think of the West as beginning at the Mississippi River and extending to the Pacific Ocean, though many people claim that California is a different and separate land. And, north to south, the West ranges from the Mexico-Texas border on the south to Canada in the north—the northern borders of Washington, Montana, North Dakota, and Minnesota. This broad definition of the West includes such states as Minnesota, Iowa, Missouri, and Arkansas, where the flavor of life is more Midwestern than Western, and Louisiana, which is traditionally a part of the Old South. For this book about the extraordinary women of the American West, the first states west of the Mississippi have been considered Midwestern, so their women are left out. Theirs is a separate story with its own excitement, adventure, and opportunities.

The factor that binds the remaining states together as the American West is the sense of challenge about the life there. It may seem that the state of Washington, with its abundant rainfall, lush growth, and cool temperatures, has little relation to Arizona, where heat and drought are common, but the American West is a land of extremes—extremes in geography as well as climate. And it is a land that challenges those who would live there.

The West has landscapes of unsurpassed grandeur—the Grand Canyon, the Rocky Mountains, the redwood forests of California, the majestic beauty of the Columbia River Gorge, and the wonder of the Arizona desert in bloom. But it is also harsh and hostile—a land of droughts, blizzards, tornadoes, and, too often, of unrelenting, blazing heat. Most of all, even today it is a land of open space and big sky.

Sacajawea

Indian Guide and Interpreter
1787?–1812? or 1888?

On their 1804–1806 expedition, Meriwether Lewis and William Clark traveled across Louisiana Territory, the northwest range of the Rockies, and on to the Pacific Northwest. Their exploration cleared the way for the countless wagon trains that followed and brought a new era to American history. It was a stunning achievement, but Lewis and Clark couldn't have done it without the help of one woman.

She was a sixteen-year-old Shoshoni Indian named Sacajawea. Lewis and Clark had hired Toussaint Charbonneau, a French-Canadian trapper known for his ability to communicate with the river tribes. When he joined the expedition's winter camp on the Missouri River, he brought two Indian women with him—"squars" as Clark's journal described them. Sacajawea, Charbonneau's wife, was also expecting a child, which she delivered well before spring when the expedition moved westward. The baby, a boy, was christened Jean Baptiste but nicknamed Pomp, a Shoshoni word meaning "first-born."

Sacajawea had been kidnapped five years earlier by a party of Hidatsa raiders and she was later traded or sold to Charbonneau. She knew both the language and the land of the Shoshoni—or the Snakes as they were often called—and she proved to be much more important to the expedition than her husband was.

The expedition left Fort Mandan on the Missouri River in April 1805. One of Sacajawea's earliest contributions was to keep the company supplied with roots and berries, an important addition to their diet. When one of the pirogues (a native canoe, usually hollowed from the trunk of a tree) overturned, it was Sacajawea who kept her head and saved many irreplaceable supplies.

Sacajawea walked with her baby strapped on her back. By mid-July, she recognized the country they were crossing and assured Lewis and Clark that they would soon be in the land of the Shoshoni. Lewis pressed ahead, leaving Clark and Sacajawea and the others to follow with the equipment. Thus, Lewis and a few companions were the first to meet Sacajawea's people and their chief, Cameahwait. Though they could not communicate, Lewis persuaded the chief and a group of his people to meet with the rest of the expedition party.

The reunion between Sacajawea and her people was apparently emotional and certainly reassuring to the Shoshoni. When she was called to translate at a powwow with the chief, she recognized Cameahwait as her brother! In

Sacajawea is honored in many American cities. This statue was erected in Bismarck, North Dakota.

exchange for gifts, the Shoshoni eventually supplied the expedition with horses to take them across the Rockies.

Although she was overjoyed to have found her people again, Sacajawea chose to continue on with Lewis, Clark, and Charbonneau. Whenever the company encountered hostile Indians —Nez Percé, Flathead, or others—her presence was reassuring to them, a sign of peaceful intent. The expedition reached the Pacific Ocean on November 8, 1805. They had traveled 4,000 miles (6,400 km).

The company spent the winter on the West Coast and then returned to the Mandan village in August 1806. Lewis and Clark paid

Charbonneau for his services—a little over $500 for sixteen months!—and said good-bye to the family.

Clark had become particularly fond of Pomp and Sacajawea—he sometimes called her Janey—and later wrote to Charbonneau, "Your woman . . . deserved a greater reward for her attention and service than we had in our power to give her at the Mandans." He offered to raise and educate Pomp, and the child was brought to St. Louis some five years later. He attended school in St. Louis and in Europe, but in 1829 he returned to the American West.

According to Shoshoni tradition, Sacajawea lived to be 100 years old and was much honored by the Shoshoni. But on December 20, 1812, a fur trader at Fort Manuel on the upper Missouri River recorded that the wife of Charbonneau, "a Snake squaw, died . . . . She was the best woman of the fort, aged about 25 years."

Sacajawea is honored in many ways, even a novel has been written about her life. But perhaps her most important monument is the statue dedicated at Portland, Oregon, at the 1905 Lewis and Clark Exposition—a century after her great trip. The occasion was seen as a celebration of women's historic achievements, and the statue was dedicated by Susan B. Anthony, then one of the most famous voices for women's rights. With her was Abigail Scott Duniway of the Northwest, an even more determined champion of women's rights.

The statue shows Sacajawea in fringed buckskins, her baby on her back, her arm stretched out, forever pointing the way. "This woman," said Duniway, "was an Indian, a mother, and a slave . . . . Little did she know that she was helping to upbuild a Pacific empire. . . . In honoring her, we pay homage to thousands of uncrowned heroines whose quiet endurance and patient efforts have made possible the achievements of the world's great men."

La Tules

Gambler
1800?–1852

Few facts are known about the woman they called "La Tules," but there are plenty of stories about where she came from and how she lived. The stories illustrate how one culture can misunderstand the customs of another.

La Tules was born Maria Gertrudis Barcelo, probably in Mexico around 1800. The name "La Tules" is an affectionate short form of Gertrudis. Sometime before 1823, she traveled north to Santa Fe (then in Mexican territory, now in New Mexico), probably with her mother, brother, and sister. On June 23, 1823, she married Manuel Sisneros at the church at Tomé. The priest who performed the marriage referred to her as Doña, a title given to women of quality and high social standing. The couple had two sons, both of whom died as infants.

No one disputes that La Tules was ambitious and that she loved to gamble. She once ran games at a mining camp in the Ortiz Mountains, but by 1835 she opened a glittering salon where the rich and powerful of Santa Fe—including Governor Manuel Armijo—came to gamble.

La Tules was an expert at dealing a card game called monte. The name came from the mountain of cards left after a certain number had been dealt. She was also a shrewd businesswoman who made a fortune and enjoyed great power in a world where both power and money were usually held by men. Residents of Santa Fe gave La Tules the same respect they gave to the governor and the priests, and she was openly received in the best places in society.

At that time, Santa Fe was undergoing great change. Before Mexico's independence from Spain in 1821, all goods came to the city from Chihuahua, Mexico. When the Santa Fe Trail opened, American traders arrived in the city, bringing new goods and new ideas. They gambled for money, fame, and fun, and it wasn't unusual for a trader to lose all his profits in one night at the gambling tables and then do a wild fandango to dance away his troubles.

But many Americans objected to the gambling and some of them recorded their impressions of La Tules. Explorer Josiah Gregg was in Santa Fe in 1844 and wrote a book, *Commerce of the Prairies,* which remains an important source of information about the Santa Fe Trail. He also wrote that La Tules had come from Taos, where she was a woman of poor reputation and could not make a living. Gregg wrote with disgust that La Tules dealt cards with men, even with the governor.

Newspaperman George Wilkins Kendall of New Orleans described La Tules as French, said her name was Madame Tule or Toulouse, and that she ran a gambling house and set the local standard for fancy dress. Yet another story said she was born in Spain.

However, Susan Magoffin, granddaughter of Kentucky's first governor and the eighteen-year-old bride of a Yankee trader, was La Tules's greatest critic. Magoffin wrote that La Tules "made her living by running a house where open gambling, drinking, and smoking were enjoyed by all . . . with no thought of being socially degraded." Poet-historian Father Fray Angelico Chavez reminds us that Spanish women often smoked cornshuck cigarettes and went about with their arms bare—customs that offended Magoffin and other Yankees. Magoffin described La Tules as the "old woman with false hair and teeth."

In August 1846, when the United States Army of the West, under General Stephen Watts Kearny, occupied Santa Fe, Doña Tules befriended the American officers. She loaned them money for an expedition to Chihuahua and she is credited with exposing a conspiracy against the Army and thereby preventing a massacre.

No one knows what happened to La Tules's husband. He is not mentioned in a will she completed in 1850. She left her residence and property to her brother and sister and to two young girls who had lived with her. When she died in 1852, all of Santa Fe attended the elaborate funeral. Even then, American writers criticized La Tules, claiming the ceremony was too fancy for a woman like her and was paid for by "ill-gotten gain." But Father Chavez documents that the funeral was quite appropriate for a woman of Tules's social standing.

The life of Doña Tules is told in a novel, *The Wind Leaves No Shadow* by Ruth Laughlin Alexander, and in *Viva Santa Fe!,* a musical which was first presented in Hobbs, New Mexico, in 1991 and then at the 1992 World's Fair in Spain.

Narcissa Whitman

Missionary
1808–1847

I n 1833, some Native Americans of the Northwest visited St. Louis, Missouri, seeking to learn more about the white man's "Book of Heaven," as they called the Bible. When this story appeared in Eastern newspapers, it inspired many people to serve as Christian missionaries to Native Americans, including Narcissa Prentiss of Angelica, New York.

Then in her mid-twenties, Narcissa was still unmarried and described as a beauty. To her dismay, the church would not allow a single woman to go west as a missionary. Narcissa's only hope of fulfilling her dream was to find a husband who shared her goal.

Such a man was Marcus Whitman, a doctor and a missionary who had been to the Oregon Territory and returned east to find more workers. He and Narcissa were married on February 18, 1836, and left immediately for the Pacific Northwest. It was a long and difficult journey—the women traveled by wagon, boat, and, most often, by riding a horse sidesaddle, a difficult thing even under good conditions.

Eventually they arrived at the fur trappers' rendezvous, an annual event held from 1824 to 1839 at which trappers exchanged furs for supplies brought by traders from the East. The arrival of the Whitman party, with Narcissa and her traveling companion, Eliza Spalding, threw confusion into the usually rough and rowdy event. They were the first white women some trappers had seen in over twelve years and the first ever seen by some American Indian men. No Anglo women before then had crossed the United States by land—most who had gone to California before had done so by a long and difficult sea journey. The Whitmans' wagon was the first vehicle to travel west over the Rockies. The Indians called it a "horse canoe."

The Whitman party continued through the Rocky Mountains, establishing a mission at Waiilatpu, a Cayuse Indian community some 6 miles (10 km) from present-day Walla Walla, Washington. *Waiilatpu* means "place of the people of the rye grass."

Narcissa Whitman gave birth to a daughter, Alice Clarissa, shortly after arriving at Waiilatpu. The day after the birth, the Cayuse crowded curiously around the baby to see the first white child born west of the Rocky Mountains. Unfortunately, Alice drowned when she was a little over two years old, but in the following years, the Whitmans adopted several children. Their family included seven children left homeless by the death of their missionary parents, as well as several Cayuse children. Whitman enjoyed raising the children and taught them about everything from Christianity to wildflowers.

But with the Cayuse, things did not go as smoothly. The Cayuse were not enthusiastic about Dr. Whitman's ideas. It was their custom to travel each year to the buffalo grounds and salmon fisheries to find food for their people. Dr. Whitman felt he could not teach them Christianity if they moved around all the time, so he encouraged them to farm instead of hunt. He had little success. Also, the Cayuse were not very interested in Dr. Whitman's religious worship, books, and school. The Whitmans, believing strongly that Christianity and their way of doing things was right, were unable to understand the Cayuse point of view.

The Cayuse were also growing alarmed about the numbers of white settlers coming from the East. As leaders of the first wagon train to the Columbia River area in Oregon, the Whitmans had encouraged westward expansion. Many white families followed them, and the Indians were afraid of losing their land.

The bad feelings between the Cayuse and the missionaries came to a head when a group of immigrants unknowingly brought a measles epidemic to the settlement. The Whitmans' white children survived the illness while many of the Cayuse people died. Rumors circulated among the Cayuse that the Whitmans were spreading poison in the air.

On November 29, 1847, the Whitmans and twelve others—including some of their adopted children—were killed by the Cayuse, under the leadership of Chief Tilaukait and a tribal leader named Tomahas. Narcissa Whitman was the only woman killed. Other women missionaries—and several children—were taken captive and held for a month until a ransom was paid.

Today, a 27-foot (8-m) monument to the Whitmans stands on a hill overlooking the site of their mission. The hill, now called Shaft Hill, had great significance in Whitman's life. Fond of flowers, she encouraged her foster children to grow flower gardens and often took them to the hill to point out wild blue flax, fiddleneck, lupine, gray and green rabbitbrush, wheatgrass, and squirrel grass. In later years, her foster children remembered the hill as the family's favorite picnic spot.

There, too, Whitman often stood watching for her husband to return from work among neighboring tribes. After the Whitman massacre, the Cayuse used the hill to keep a lookout for intruders while they held the massacre survivors for ransom. Today, thousands of visitors climb to the top of the hill each year to see the monument to the Whitmans, which reads in part, "In patience, courage and endurance, women proved man's equal."

Narcissa Whitman's story is well known because of the violence of her death, but she was also the first Anglo woman to live in the Pacific Northwest and her presence opened the way for many to follow.

The Indian Captives

More than anything else, frontier women feared capture by Indians. Some captives who were returned to white civilization, either by rescue or ransom, wrote about their experiences or toured through cities and gave lectures. They caught the public interest in a horrifying way. Those few who made their experience public received so much attention that people back East believed women were captured by the hundreds. Actually, though many pioneer women were killed in conflicts with the Indians, not as many were taken captive as was generally believed.

Perhaps the best-known memoir of an Indian captive is Fanny Kelly's *Narrative of My Captivity among the Sioux Indians.* Fanny Kelly was nineteen years old and married nine months in 1864 when she and her husband and her five-year-old stepdaughter, Mary, set out with a handful of immigrants from Wyoming's Fort Laramie. The army had declared that the journey was safe, but the small group had gone less than 80 miles (129 km) when they were attacked by 250 Oglala Sioux Indians. Although Fanny's husband escaped, most men of the party were killed. Fanny and Mary were captured along with the other women and children. Mary was later killed after trying to escape.

Most white women swore they would prefer death to captivity, but not Fanny. She held on to the hope of rescue throughout her ordeal. Every time the Indians tried to tattoo her, as was their custom, she fainted. They might have killed her as a coward had she not, in an extraordinary act of bravery, saved another white woman who was about to be killed because she cried all the time. Ottawa, a chief, was impressed, and Fanny became his property.

Fanny Kelly

Death threatened Fanny regularly during her captivity. Once, she carelessly discarded a peace pipe Ottawa had given her to guard. The chief decided to put her to death for this sacrilege. As Fanny was about to be tied to an unbroken horse and then shot full of arrows, she had an inspiration. She took out her purse and gave the braves all her paper money—about $120. They were so interested in the money and its value that they began questioning Fanny and forgot about killing her.

In the Oglala camp, Fanny survived by obedience, cheerfulness, and hard work. The Indians even called her "Real Woman," because, she later wrote, she set an example of the way they thought women should behave. Indian women were often rebellious because they were treated like servants.

The Sioux grew fond of Fanny and were reluctant to release her, in spite of pressure from the army. Fanny Kelly became a political prize. When she was acquired by Blackfeet Sioux, Fanny suspected they wanted to use her to attack Fort Sully. She smuggled a letter to the army by means of a young love-struck Indian named Jumping Bear. Finally, accompanied by 1,000 mounted warriors, she was peacefully returned to the white settlement in exchange for three horses and a load of food supplies.

Olive Oatman was another woman who gathered fame from her captivity. In 1851, when she was thirteen or fourteen years old, her family headed for California with a wagon train. When her father recklessly moved his wagon ahead of the others, the lone wagon was attacked by Yavapai Indians in the Gila River Valley in Arizona Territory. Only Olive and her sister, Mary Ann, survived, and they were carried off to be slaves.

This photograph of Olive Oatman shows the tattoo marks made on her face during her time in captivity.

A year later, the girls were sold to the Mojave Indians, who walked them north to the Colorado River. During a drought in 1853, Mary Ann died. The Mojave put their mark on Olive as they did to their own women—they tattooed her chin, jawline, and arms.

Olive was not as alone in the world as she thought, however. Her brother Lorenzo, left for dead at the scene of the attack, survived and made his way to safety. His five-year search for his sister finally ended with a Yuma Indian who knew about Olive and arranged for her release—for a fee.

Olive Oatman returned to Fort Yuma, but it took several months for her to learn to live in white society again. In time, she lectured in several cities, recounting the stories of her captivity and letting people stare at her tattooed face. Eventually, she married.

But Olive Oatman was marked for life, both physically, by the tattoos, and emotionally, by her experiences. She was once described as set apart from the world by her sufferings.

Perhaps the best-known and most-written-about captive was young Cynthia Ann Parker of Texas. Cynthia Ann was only nine years old in 1836 when a band of Comanche, Kiowa, and Caddo Indians—some say between 500 and 800 warriors—attacked the fort where she lived with her large family of grandparents, parents, uncles, aunts, and cousins. Most were massacred, a few escaped, and some, like Cynthia Ann, were captured. Their fates varied from ransom and rescue to death in captivity.

Proving herself tough, Cynthia Ann was adopted by the Comanche and lived among them for twenty-five years, marrying a chief named Peta Nocona and bearing him three children. Several ransom attempts, undertaken at the request of her brother, who had also been a captive, were refused. Cynthia Ann did not want to leave her adopted people.

In December 1860, the Texas Rangers were on the trail of the Comanche, who had been raiding in North Central Texas. The Rangers arrived at a camp on the Pease River when the Comanche men were off hunting; women, children, and male slaves were in the camp. As the Indians, blanketed against the cold, tried to escape, several were killed. Cynthia Ann would have been shot too had not her blanket blown away to reveal that she was a woman, carried a child in her arms, and had blonde hair (although greased in the Comanche style) and blue eyes.

She was questioned by Isaac Parker, a former senator in the Congress of the Republic of Texas. He got no answers from her until, in disgust, he said, "My niece's name was Cynthia Ann." Then the "Indian" woman patted herself on the breast and said, "Me Cyncee Ann."

Cynthia Ann and her daughter, Prairie Flower, stayed with various Parker relatives, but she was always unhappy, always hoping to return to those she now considered her people. Her

Cynthia Ann Parker

husband, Peta Nocona, had been killed on the Pease River, but, longing for her son, Quanah, she tried to escape several times and was always returned to "civilization."

In 1864, Prairie Flower died of a fever, and Cynthia Ann, grieving in the Comanche manner, starved herself to death. In Fort Worth, Texas, visitors may wander through the Parker cabin in which she spent the last years of her life.

Her son, Quanah Parker, became a leader of the Comanche and helped his people face their defeat at the hands of the U.S. Army and learn to "walk on the white man's road." He is considered a hero by many, and Cynthia Ann's romantic and tragic story is still remembered.

The Years of Adventure

Custer and his men are overwhelmed at the Battle of Little Bighorn.

In 1861, before the Civil War's first shots were fired, the people of the American West saw eastern ways of life creeping into their lands. For the Spanish settlements in California, it was the rough miners of the 1849 Gold Rush. In Texas, Stephen F. Austin and others led a successful rebellion against the Mexican government and established the Republic of Texas, clearly a white government. The Plains Indians watched in horror and puzzlement as buffalo hunters destroyed the great herds that provided food and all the necessities of life for the Indian. Hunters, trappers, mountain men, and traders filtered into the Northwest to explore its magnificent mountains and live off its animals.

Even so, white settlement of the West was relatively sparse and survival overshadowed every other concern. Both men and women were constantly threatened by disease, extreme weather, and the constant danger of Indian attack. After the Civil War, however, life in the American West changed dramatically.

During the war, both the North and the South were too occupied with battle to pay much attention to the West and what was called "the Indian problem." The Plains Indians—the Sioux, Comanche, Cheyenne, and others—grew bold, attacking white settlements frequently and often viciously, knowing there were no soldiers to follow the raiding parties and fight back.

After the Union victory, however, the United States found itself with a large army and brilliant generals with no battles to fight. The government decided to send them west to deal with "the Indian problem." The years that followed saw several landmark battles—the Battle of Washita, the Sand Creek Massacre, the defeat and capture of Chief Joseph and his Nez Percé tribe, and many others. The last great Indian victory came in 1876 in the Montana Territory when the Sioux, under Sitting Bull, massacred General George Armstrong Custer and his men at the Battle of the Little Bighorn.

By then, "the Indian problem" was pretty much over, and settlers no longer had to live in fear.

These years also saw the great cattle drives. During the war, Texas ranchers let their cattle roam wild in the brush of south Texas. After the war, many men made a fortune by rounding up those cattle and driving them to markets in Kansas. The Longhorn—tough, stringy cattle, suffered very little during the long journey and brought a good price. We think of cattle drives as a basic part of the Old West, but they lasted barely twenty years. The land was then so fenced in and settled that a cattle drive was nearly impossible, and in any case, the growth of the railroads made shipping more practical.

During these years—1865–1900—settlers were no longer intruders. Having forced the American Indians onto reservations and greatly outnumbering the Hispanic population, the settlers were the people who lived on the land. They built communities and women brought white civilization, as they knew it, to these small and large towns. They established schools, churches, literary societies, sewing groups, and charitable organizations. They brought the latest fashions from the East—maybe a year or two out of date, but no longer simply the poke bonnet and the gingham dress. They raised their children, planted their flower gardens, and tried hard to re-create eastern society in the American West.

As the West was settled, more and more women came. Many came alone, some in search of husbands and others simply looking for new lives and new freedom. Although most women chose traditional roles as laundresses, cooks, and teachers, many became shopkeepers, restaurateurs, lawyers, doctors, dentists, journalists, pawnbrokers, actresses, barbers, photographers, and even mule skinners and outlaws. A surprising number of women came to homestead and "prove up" land so that they could own it (to "prove up" land meant to improve it by building a dwelling on it). After the Civil War, the West was the land of opportunity for women.

A wagon train of settlers moves west.

These women, like their men, went west chasing the dream of a new life. The American West at the turn of the last century was a fine land of opportunity for women. We think of careers and divorce as unusual in that day and age because we tend to think of eastern models—women who lived in New York, Ohio, or Virginia. These women simply didn't have the freedom of choice. They were bound by a society and conventions that didn't affect their sisters in the West. Women who took advantage of the freedom of the West were also distinguished by a sense of hope. They looked to the bright future that the land of opportunity offered them.

Esther Morris

Champion of Women's Rights
1814–1902

In 1869, a western territory—Wyoming—was the first to give American women suffrage—or the right to vote. And though men gave women the right to vote, it was one woman—Esther Morris—who made it happen. In Wyoming, she is known as the "Mother of Woman's Suffrage."

Esther Morris was an unlikely heroine. Born in Spencer, New York, in 1814, and orphaned at a young age, she earned a living doing housework for neighbors. Later, she opened a millinery shop because she loved beautiful things, especially flowers, and enjoyed decorating hats with them. In 1841, she married a railroad man and moved with him to Illinois. Her husband's early death made Esther aware of the problems of women's rights: she had no rights over his property or over their only child, a son.

In 1845 she married John Morris, a storekeeper. Some twenty years later, Esther followed Morris and their three sons to the goldfields at South Pass, Wyoming. In those twenty years, she had worked for the antislavery movement, and she had been aware of the battle for women's rights.

As early as 1848, Eastern feminists had met at Seneca Falls, New York, and published a list of rights to which women were entitled. The right to vote was among them. But tradition dictated that only men may vote, and for the next twenty-one years women continued to be denied that right.

Esther Morris knew that in the East things were often done the way they had always been done because people feared change. She saw the West as a new land where traditions had not yet been established. The political climate was more open.

Esther decided to campaign for the right to vote. She started with a tea party. Morris was not the kind of woman you associate with tea parties, being almost 6 feet (183 cm) tall and well built, with a plain face and an even plainer manner of speaking. In South Pass, she was known for her nursing skills and for the colorful garden around her small house. But she was not known for tea parties.

The story goes that she invited the only two candidates for the state legislature to tea, seeking their pledge that they would support the right to vote for women. Some say both men agreed but others say only William H. Bright agreed. He eventually won the election. Bright was sympathetic because Morris had saved the life of his wife in a difficult childbirth. Still another version is that Mrs. Bright herself was a suffragette and Bright, who had moved west from Virginia, saw no reason why his wife should not vote when that privilege was given to former slaves.

Esther Morris lived in this cabin at South Pass, Montana.

When the legislature met, Bright introduced the bill, and although there was some grumbling, it passed. Wyoming at that time had very few women residents, and the legislators may have believed the bill would draw attention to the state and encourage more women to settle there. The bill also provided that women could own property, earn and keep money, serve on juries, and be the guardians of minor children—rights that had been denied until then. The governor signed the bill into law, and the legislators are supposed to have raised a toast: "Lovely ladies, once our superiors, now our equals."

In 1870 in South Pass, Morris was appointed the world's first female justice of the peace. This caused lots of laughter back East, where the newspapers were full of jokes and cartoons about a female justice of the peace. But Morris did her job well. She held court in a log cabin and ordered guns left outside the door. The story goes that when her saloon-keeper husband, John, objected to her new position and made a scene, she fined him. When he refused to pay the fine, she sent him to jail. In slightly over seven months, Esther Morris ruled on seventy cases, and none were overturned on appeal. She did not seek office when her term expired because she had made her point—a woman could be an effective justice of the peace.

In 1870, the Laramie, Wyoming, court called the first jury that included women. Newspaper reporters from the East came to the trial to make fun of the women, but the judge supported his jurors and the trial proceeded smoothly. Esther Morris's actions were having an effect.

Meanwhile, the fight for women's rights went on across the nation, and the western states were in the lead in giving the vote to women. By the time women's suffrage was added to the U. S. Constitution in 1920, women throughout the West, except in Texas and New Mexico, were already voting.

In 1892, when she was seventy-eight years old, Esther Morris was elected a delegate to the National Republican Convention in Cleveland, Ohio, and officially cast Wyoming's votes for Benjamin Harrison. When she died in 1902, her son said, "The work she did for the elevation of womankind will be told in the years to come, when the purpose will be better understood."

The log cabin at South Pass where she held her tea party—and later held court—has been restored, with a plaque citing both Morris and W. H. Bright. In 1955, the Wyoming legislature ordered a 9-foot (2.7-m) bronze statue of Morris to be placed in the Wyoming niche in the U. S. Capitol Building in Washington, D.C. It bears the words "Mother of Equal Rights."

Sally Skull

Smuggler
1817?–1866?

Sally Skull's story might be told along with those of other outlaw women—Calamity Jane and Belle Starr—but she never had the national reputation those two women gained. She is a legend on the Texas-Mexico border but not well known elsewhere. Sally Skull was, in her own way, a Civil War heroine. Many women on both sides risked their lives during that war, but few of them operated west of the Mississippi River. Sally Skull was a Confederate heroine from Texas.

Facts about her life are hard to come by. She was born Sarah Jane Newman and probably came to Texas with her family when she was six years old. Sally married early, perhaps as young as thirteen, but her parents had that marriage anulled. She married again—and not much later—to Jesse Robinson, who owned land and horses, although he was only in his early twenties. They had three children—Alfred, Nancy, and a baby who died in infancy.

That marriage lasted until 1842, when the couple divorced. The children stayed with their father, and Sally began ranching in Nueces County in south

Texas. Nobody knows how she got the money to establish her ranch, but she traded horses in Mexico, often crossing the border alone, armed with a whip and a pistol.

Her experience enabled her to help the Confederacy. When Union forces blockaded the Texas seaports and supplies could not reach either soldiers or civilians, Sally traded horses in Mexico for guns, ammunition, medicine, coffee, shoes, clothing, and other necessary items.

Friends recalled Sally as trustworthy and fearless. She dressed flamboyantly and rode a magnificent horse, Redbuck, with a silver-trimmed saddle. That, her friends said, was simply the way to do business in Mexico. And dancing at village fiestas? That was how she became friends with the Mexicans, even the dreaded bandito Juan Cortina, who allowed her to enter his territory without trouble. Many recalled her acts of kindness—a crock of butter left on the doorstep of a poor household, a new dress for a child, a risk taken to lead others across a flood-swollen river.

But gossip swirled about Sally too. A blue-eyed blonde who wore a thick money belt, she drank, played poker, and a was known for her colorful vocabulary. Once she came upon a preacher whose horses were mired in the mud. His gentle urgings did nothing to move the animals. Sally let loose with a stream of curses, and the horses leaped into action. Soon, the horses bogged down again, and the preacher turned to Sally and said, "Please, ma'am, would you speak to my horses again?"

She was said to have married three more times—once to George Skull, whose name she kept, probably to Watkins Doyle, and again to Bill Horsdoff. Rumor said she once killed a man in an old-fashioned shootout, facing him down and drawing first. She could twirl her guns like a man and come up shooting. She dressed like a man and rode astride, rather than sidesaddle like proper women of her time. And, supposedly, she shot one husband and drowned another.

The truth about Sally will probably never be known—not even what happened to her in the end. Sally was never seen after about 1866, when she would have been about forty-nine years old. Sally and her last husband—Bill Horsdoff—did not get along, and he was said to be a "hard case." Some say that Horsdoff shot her on a trading trip to Mexico and buried her body. If so, it was the first time anyone outsmarted—or outdrew—Sally Skull.

Sally Skull is barely remembered as a Confederate heroine, and she didn't lead a model life by any standards. But her daring and courage make her an extraordinary woman of the American West.

Mother Joseph

Good Samaritan
1823–1902

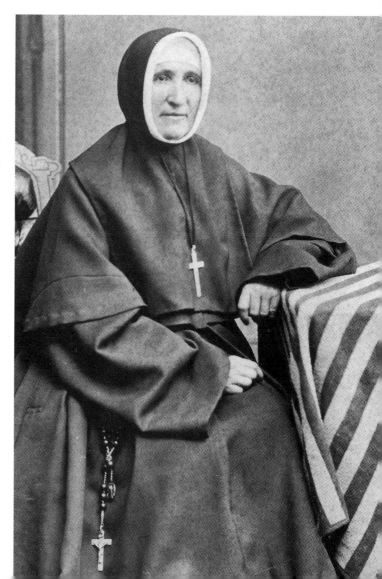

Mother Joseph, a member of the order of Roman Catholic nuns known as the Sisters of Providence, was among the first people in the Northwest to care for orphans, the aged, and the mentally ill. She was also the first to establish a hospital and a permanent Catholic school.

Mother Joseph was born Esther Pariseau in Montreal, Canada, the daughter of a carriage maker who taught her to use an adze, saw, rasp, level, plane, and chisel. When she was twenty and decided to enter a religious order, her father told the supervisor at the convent: "I bring you my daughter, Esther, who wishes to dedicate herself to the religious life. She can cook, sew, and spin, and do all manner of housework. She has learned carpentry from me and she will someday make a very good superior."

The new nun served in Montreal until 1856, when she and four others made the difficult journey to Fort Vancouver in the far Northwest Territory. Their new home was a small unfinished attic. Within days, Mother Joseph had remodeled the room so that it had a dormitory for sleeping, a community room, a dining area, and a small classroom.

In February 1857, the sisters were given their first convent—an old fur-storage building that had been abandoned by the Hudson's Bay Company and later used as a barn. Mother Joseph designed the chapel in this building and built the altar herself.

Fort Vancouver was not an easy place to establish a religious community. Both Fort Vancouver, a military outpost, and the city of Portland, Oregon, across the Columbia River, were tough towns where people were more concerned with lumber, shipping, mining and trade, than with their souls. In addition, most residents were English-speaking Protestants. The French-speaking nuns were alone and homesick in the harsh, wet climate of the Pacific Coast.

They asked for spindles and spinning wheels, so that they could make their own warm woolen clothes at less cost. They visited the sick in their homes and cared for Yakima children, who had been displaced in the recent Indian wars.

By June, Mother Joseph had built six small cabins surrounded by a white fence. The cluster of buildings became known as the "Providence enclosure." The sisters established a boarding school and took in orphans. They also taught day students and cared for elderly townspeople.

Mother Joseph was building a bakery-laundry cabin when a priest talked to her about the community's desperate need for a hospital. He told of one young man, dying of tuberculosis, who had no place to stay. If Mother Joseph would oversee construction, the Ladies of Charity Volunteer Group would finance and manage the hospital. Mother Joseph set aside her work on the bakery-laundry and adapted the building into a hospital with space for four beds, four tables, and four chairs. It became known as Saint Joseph Hospital—the first of some two dozen health centers she would design in her forty-six years in the Northwest.

Not all projects came easily. In 1866, Mother Joseph had converted an old house into the first asylum for the mentally ill, but she was unable to keep the building open because of lack of money. The people of Vancouver now supported her projects, but they were poor people with little money to donate to charity. Mother Joseph decided to appeal to the gold miners who were getting rich in Montana and Idaho. She went to the mining camps herself and appealed to the miners while the gold was still in their pockets, before they could spend it in nearby towns.

These "begging tours" must have seemed foolish and dangerous to others, but Mother Joseph was clever. Knowing her own limitations—she was a large woman who sometimes scared others, had an abrupt manner, and spoke only broken English—she took a younger, prettier sister with her. The tours usually lasted several months, and the nuns endured cold weather, slept in tents or stagecoaches, and survived occasional stagecoach robberies. They confronted roustabouts, miners, and other "get-rich-quick" vagabonds. They entered dark mining tunnels several hundred feet underground. On one trip, Mother Joseph wrote in her journal, she encountered a hungry wolf pack, an angry grizzly bear, and a party of Indians in war paint. Also on that trip, their tent caught fire!

But Mother Joseph usually returned to Vancouver with anywhere from $2,000 to $5,000, a very large sum in those days.

As early as 1861, Mother Joseph saw the need for permanent buildings for education, medicine, and missionary care. But it was twelve years before she could lay the cornerstone for the House of Providence, a three-story brick building on 2 acres (0.8 hectare) of ground. One newspaper reported that it was the largest brick building in the state of Washington. The nuns moved into the house in September 1873 and by 1889 the building was too small for their work.

When it was evident that a new hospital was needed, a businessman offered to build it on land he owned. After much prayer, Mother Joseph rejected the businessman's offer. She believed the hospital would have served the businessman, who had a shady reputation, but would not have met the most urgent health needs of the people. Soon, the Society of St. Vincent de Paul came forward with $1,000 and a better piece of land. Mother Joseph designed the first St.

Vincent Hospital, which opened in July 1875, and even carved the statue of its patron saint at the entrance. In 1892, she designed another larger hospital that bore the same name.

In 1887, when she was sixty-four years old, Mother Joseph insisted on living in a rough shack next to the construction site of the Sacred Heart Hospital in Spokane, Washington. She was still climbing to inspect rafters or bouncing on planks to test their supports. On one occasion, she pointed out to workers that a chimney had been improperly laid. They ignored her but returned the next day to find the chimney had been rebricked.

Mother Joseph died in 1902 of a brain tumor. A local newspaper said she had established eleven hospitals, seven academies, five Indian schools, and two orphanages. In 1952, the American Institute of Architects honored her as the "First Architect of the Northwest." Because she was among the first to appreciate the use of the Douglas fir, native to that region, for both carving and building, she was honored by the West Coast Lumberman's Association. And in 1980, the state of Washington gave her national attention when her statue was placed in the state's niche in Statuary Hall in the U. S. Capitol. She was the first woman from the Northwest and the first Catholic nun represented in this official gallery of America's "first citizens."

Jessie Benton Frémont

Senator's Daughter, Explorer's Wife
1824–1902

essie Benton Frémont was the daughter of Thomas Hart Benton, a United States senator from Missouri, and the wife of John Charles Frémont, explorer, map-maker, soldier of fortune, presidential candidate, governor, and mining king. But neither man would have gone down in history without Jessie.

She was born at Cherry Grove, her mother's plantation home near Lexington, Virginia, on May 31, 1824. Most of her childhood was spent in Washington, D.C., where as a young child she was on familiar terms with presidents, senators, and diplomats. From her earliest days, Jessie loved to spend time in her father's study, looking at his books, tracing his maps with her fingers, and listening to him talk.

She was less happy about time spent in boarding school, but her pleas to come home were ignored. Finally, in anger, she chopped off her hair. She was then allowed to return home, where she quickly became her father's assistant. She also acted as his hostess since her mother was an invalid. Jessie was an excellent hostess who could talk easily and knowledgeably about the politics of the day.

John Charles Frémont was often a dinner guest at the Benton home. Thomas Benton liked to talk to the young man about his explorations of the West, because he too believed that the flag of the United States should wave from coast to coast. But Benton did not like Frémont's attraction to Jessie— nor hers to him. He thought Jessie was too young to marry and, besides, he did not think Frémont could offer her the kind of life Benton wanted for her. But it was obvious that the two were in love. Benton made them promise to wait a year before they thought about marriage.

Instead, they ran away to marry. Benton was furious and refused to recognize the marriage, but eventually father and daughter made peace. The young couple moved into the Benton home, and Jessie was once again her father's assistant. Frémont was soon put in charge of an expedition to explore the territory beyond the Missouri River. He found a route over the Rocky Mountains and returned home in triumph, just days before Jessie gave birth to a daughter named Lily. She was bitterly disappointed that she had not presented her husband with a son.

Frémont had to write a report of his expedition, but every time he sat down, he could not write about what he had seen. Jessie helped him. He dictated the report to her, and she wrote it. Praise for his report was so great that Frémont was soon sent on an expedition to survey the Pacific.

When he left in the spring of 1843, Jessie and Lily went with him to St. Louis, her father's home. Frémont had requested and received a small cannon to protect his men. After he left, Jessie opened his mail and found a demand that he return to Washington immediately to explain the need for the cannon. Instead of sending her husband the message, she sent him a note that said only, "Make haste, do not ask why—only go."

John was expected home in eight months; but he was gone more than a year. Jessie was frantic with worry. She received no direct messages but heard that he had a hard time crossing the Sierra mountains. He finally returned, tired but triumphant, and once again the report of the trip, written together, made him a hero. John Frémont had opened the West to settlement; but it would never have happened if he had not followed Jessie's advice to make haste and go.

His third expedition was to survey Oregon and secure California for the United States. He left in 1844. In 1846, the Mexicans ordered him to leave California. Instead, he attacked a Mexican fort at Sonoma and raised a flag with a bear on it. The event is now called the Bear Flag Revolt. Frémont claimed he had the authority to take this action; but the army denied it. He returned in disgrace, was court-martialed, found guilty of disobedience, and resigned from the army. Jessie was expecting another baby, and the trial was hard on her health.

Next, Frémont went on a privately funded expedition to California. Jessie and the children accompanied him as far as a fort on the Missouri River, but the baby, sickly from birth, died on the trip. The grieving Jessie planned to join John in California, and she and Lily took a ship from New York to the Isthmus of Panama (now the Panama Canal). Panama was hot, dirty, and full of disease; it was also full of men trying to get to California to seek gold. No ships returned from California because the crews jumped ship to search for gold. This left armies of men stranded in Panama and it was no place for a woman and child. Jessie and Lily first boarded a small steamer, then traveled in dugout canoes, and finally crossed the 21 miles (34 km) of the isthmus on mules. Jessie made protectors out of the would-be miners.

At last, the family was reunited in California and settled in Monterrey. But John was soon elected senator from California, and they returned to Washington, D.C., once more making the dangerous crossing at Panama. In Washington, Jessie, John, and Senator Benton made enemies—including Jessie's mother's Southern family—because they were outspoken in their opposition to slavery.

When John's term expired, the Frémont family, including new baby John Charles, returned to California where John had mining interests. A fourth child, Ann, was born on a long vacation in France, but she too died five months later. In 1855, when Jessie was twenty-nine, John went on his last expedition and Jessie had her last child—a boy named Frank.

When John returned, he was asked to accept the nomination for president by the new Republican Party. Senator Benton disapproved of the Republican Party, and John's nomination caused a great rift in the family. Jessie was the first woman to be involved in a campaign, and at rallies people called for "Frémont and Jessie." They called her "Our Jessie." She handled all her husband's correspondence and appointments and became, in effect, his administrative assistant.

Frémont was defeated, and the family again returned to their mine in California. These were happy years for Jessie, as John was an active part of the family. Politics and expeditions were far away, and they lived quietly, first in the mountains and then on a cliff overlooking San Francisco Bay.

In 1861, when the Civil War broke out, Frémont was commissioned as a major general, commanding the Department of the West, and the family left for St. Louis, Missouri. Once again, Jessie handled John's correspondence and appointments, and gossips claimed that Jessie, not John, ran the

Department of the West. Frémont got into trouble with President Lincoln when he issued his own emancipation proclamation—before Lincoln's—freeing the slaves of Missouri citizens. Jessie traveled to Washington to plead with Lincoln, but he canceled John's commission and accused Jessie of meddling in men's business.

Frémont's business affairs then began to fall apart. He received less for his California mine than he had anticipated, and he lost money taking chances on railroads. They were broke, and their only income came from articles that Jessie began writing. She was paid $100 per column. Still they had to sell their house and their belongings. They had gone from greatness and richness to poverty and disgrace, but Jessie remained proud and supportive of John.

Frémont's last chance came in 1878 when he was appointed territorial governor of Arizona. The Frémonts were there four years, but John left the position in disgrace. He had paid more attention to making money in silver mines than to governing Arizona. The family moved to Los Angeles and worked on John's memoirs, *Memoirs of My Life,* which sold poorly. John Charles Frémont died in 1890.

Their oldest daughter, Lily, had never married and was her mother's companion. Jessie talked often of writing her own memoirs, but Lily discouraged her, feeling that some episodes would be too painful. Jessie Benton Frémont died in 1902. With her father and her husband, she had truly left her mark on the history of the American West.

Elisabet Ney

Sculptor
1833–1907

Elisabet Ney spent the first forty years of her life in Europe, where she achieved great success as a sculptor at a time when men dominated the world of European sculpture. But in 1872, she moved to Texas with her husband. She was eccentric and talented and she did not get along with many of her Texas neighbors, but Elisabet Ney is considered Texas's first artist, the woman credited with bringing fine art west of the Mississippi and with making western heroes the subject of art.

Ney considered this sculpture of Lady Macbeth to be her best work.

Ney was married to Edmund Montgomery, but she refused to take his name or wear a wedding ring because she thought marriage made a woman the servant of a man. However, when Ney and Montgomery and their two sons moved into Liendo, a plantation north of Houston, the folks of Waller County were suspicious. They were sure the couple were not married. The neighbors were also stunned by the strange outfits Ney wore. She dressed in either flowing Grecian gowns or white trousers—known as bloomers—with knee boots and a mannish-looking black coat.

When Ney's eldest son, her beloved "Arti," died, there was no funeral. Word spread that Ney had burned the body, instead of giving her son a Christian burial, and that she had made a death mask of the child. Supposedly, some men were ready to lynch her when Ney's lawyer explained that she had, much to her distress, burned the boy's body to prevent the spread of diphtheria—then a highly infectious disease.

For twenty years after her arrival in Texas, Ney ran the plantation and did not touch her sculpture. But Texas politician Oran Milo Roberts, later governor of the state, remembered her European reputation and sat for a bust. Through his influence, she was commissioned to do statues of Texas heroes Stephen F. Austin and Sam Houston for the World's Columbian Exposition in Chicago in 1893. She declined to accept the pay and requested only materials for her sculpture.

Ney moved to Austin where she hoped to open a school of sculpture and to experience an intellectual atmosphere that did not exist in Liendo. She bought land in a fashionable part of town and pitched a tent until her studio was ready. Many of Austin's most famous people called on her in this tent.

The Austin studio, called Formosa, was completed in 1891, when Ney was fifty-nine years old, and she began work on the statues. In those days, it was usual for statues to show figures in flowing Grecian gowns or in the stove-pipe hat and long coat of the day. Ney dressed Houston in a solder's uniform while Austin was clad in buckskins, cradling a rifle and holding a map of Texas. Today, both marble statues are in the Texas State capitol, with copies in the National Statuary Hall in the Capitol in Washington, D.C.

When the statues were installed in the Capitol, someone complained about the difference in their sizes—Austin a mere "scrap" of a man and Houston towering at 6 feet 2 inches (188 cm). Ney replied that God had made the two men, and she had merely reproduced their likenesses. Any dissatisfaction should be taken up with God.

The statues made Ney famous in Texas, and she soon had other commissions. She made sculptures of Texas heroes, including Lawrence "Sul"

Sullivan Ross, the Texas Ranger who rescued the Indian captive Cynthia Ann Parker. She also did a likeness of General Albert Sidney Johnston, a heroic Texas cavalry officer and Confederate general killed in the Civil War.

But the piece into which Ney put her heart was a figure of Shakespeare's Lady Macbeth, guilt-ridden after the death of King Duncan. Ney felt this sculpture, capturing guilt and inner agony, was her masterpiece, and she was so moved by it that she kept it covered most of the time and looked at it only for a few minutes a day. In ill health for some time, she died in June 1907 and was quietly buried at Liendo.

Ney had spent half her life in the American West, but it was in some ways always a strange land to her and she was always an outsider. Nevertheless, she left a strong legacy. Formosa, her studio, was the first building in Texas specifically built for art; she was the first artist of international training and reputation to live in the West; and her biography was the first art-related book written and published in Texas. In 1911, the Elisabet Ney Museum was founded at Formosa, where it is maintained today by the city of Austin and attracts thousands of visitors and students each year.

Mary Fields

Housekeeper, Restaurateur, Mail Carrier, and Laundress
1832–1914

Mary Fields was one of Montana's greatest characters. A former slave, she stood 6 feet (182 cm) tall, weighed 200 pounds (90 kg), liked to smoke cigars, and was once said to be as "black as a burnt-over prairie." She usually had a pistol strapped under her apron and a jug of whiskey by her side.

Born in Tennessee and freed by Lincoln's 1863 Emancipation Proclamation, Fields worked in the home of Judge Edmund Dunne. When the judge's wife died, Mary took the

Abigail Scott Duniway

Women's Rights Advocate
1834–1915

It was a personal triumph for Abigail Scott Duniway when, in 1912, Oregon became the seventh state to allow women to vote. For forty-two years, she had fought and suffered hardships and public ridicule to win this victory for women.

Abigail Scott was born into a poor Illinois farm family on October 22, 1834. Her mother, Ann, was so overworked that she had little time for Abigail, and her father, Tucker Scott, was clearly disappointed that the baby was a girl. As a child, Abigail was sickly but nonetheless expected to carry her share of the load. She remembered standing on chairs to wash dishes, paring huge piles of apples, and cleaning wool fleece. She attended school only occasionally and was known as the most independent of the Scott children.

By the late 1840s, Tucker Scott had the itch to follow the wagon trains west. When the Oregon Land Donation Act passed in 1850, giving 320 acres (130 hectares) to every settler and another 320 to his wife, Abigail's father decided to move his family to Oregon. Abigail's mother had borne nine more children, and over the years she had become a semi-invalid. She did not survive the hardships of the wagon train trip, and neither did one of her young sons. The family left two graves on the trail to Oregon.

Once in Oregon, Abigail's father soon remarried. Every unmarried man in Oregon wanted to marry to get the second 320 acres (130 hectares) of land, and Abigail herself was courted by several men. But she was still independent and knew she didn't want to marry a dominating man like her father. She married Benjamin C. Duniway, because he loved her and didn't marry her for the land.

They farmed in a fairly remote area, and Abigail found herself repeating her mother's life—cooking, washing, cleaning, and bearing children. She raised chickens and churned butter, but Ben kept the money. Abigail called their farm Hardscrabble.

In 1855 the family moved to a new farm, where they were closer to neighbors and Abigail had more companionship and less work. She called this home Sunny Hillside.

In 1859, when she was twenty-five, Abigail published a novel called *Captain Gray's Company, or Crossing the Plains and Living in Oregon.* It was the first novel published in Oregon, but it was a failure. Critics said too many of the characters were overworked women! Abigail next began writing a column, "The Farmer's Wife," for the *New Oregon Farmer.* Again, she was criticized for writing too often of the hardships of a farmer's wife.

Abigail became more aware of women's issues and politics when her husband signed a note for a friend. The friend could not pay, and Abigail found that she was as responsible for the debt as Ben was, even though she had begged him not to sign it. They lost Sunny Hillside farm and had to move to a house in the town of Lafayette. Abigail opened a small school and took boarding students into their home. She rose early to do chores, then taught school all day. Ben started a hauling business, but it was not a success. Then he was injured when he was thrown under the wheels of a wagon; he was a semi-invalid for the rest of his life.

To support her family, Abigail sold the school—it was more work than she could handle—and opened a millinery or hat-making business. In her store, she began to hear the stories of other women: one woman's husband took all their money and belongings and left town and another husband used the butter money to buy a race horse instead of the waterproof children's coats for which it was intended. Another woman said her husband had died but the court would not let her use the money from his estate to support their children. Abigail began to write again, using her pen to tell these women's stories.

When Ben said that women would never be better off until they could vote, Abigail found her purpose in life. She would work to get the vote for women. Deciding to publish a newspaper for women, she moved her family—there were now six children—to Portland and produced *The New Northwest*. Her sons ran the business, while she did the writing.

When two famous suffragettes, Susan B. Anthony and Elizabeth Cady Stanton, were speaking in the West, Abigail invited them to Portland. Because many places refused to welcome a suffragette lecture, Abigail rented a hall. Ben collected tickets, and one of their daughters provided the music. After the meeting, Abigail went with Anthony on a tour of Oregon. They spoke in halls, saloons, and churches, and their topic was always the same—injustice to women. Most wives, they said, were more or less slaves.

Back home again, Abigail campaigned for women's rights. In 1872, she introduced a suffrage bill to the Washington legislature; it did not pass. Another bill did pass, however, which allowed women to register their businesses with county clerks, thereby protecting their tools, furniture, and stock from seizure if their husbands went into debt. Abigail's newspaper would not suffer if Ben made another bad loan.

Many suffragettes associated their cause with temperance—the avoidance of alcohol. Abigail knew that would not work. Men would never support a cause that required them to stop drinking alcohol. She did not support prohibition—the outlawing of liquor—and wrote editorials saying that drinking was a physical problem, not a moral evil like the enslavement of women.

In 1883 the suffrage bill passed in Washington Territory. Abigail was sure she could make it pass in Oregon next, and she began an active campaign, reminding women that even the mentally ill and criminals could vote. Only women could not. But the bill did not pass in Oregon.

Ben Duniway became ill again, and the family moved to Idaho, hoping the country air would bring him better health. In 1896, Idaho granted women the right to vote. Ben Duniway died that year, and Abigail wrote a column about his loyalty to her and to women's causes. Then she threw herself into her work. She founded women's clubs, led parades, held rallies. Each time the Oregon suffrage bill was defeated—1906, 1908, 1910—she began all over again.

By 1911, she was seventy-seven years old and confined to a wheelchair. Arthritis, perhaps a result of her hard childhood, had crippled her. But she could still write, and other people could deliver her speeches. She said that when she died and went to heaven, she wanted to go as a free woman.

Oregon gave women the vote in 1912, and the governor invited Abigail to sign the official proclamation of the amendment to the state constitution.

At the next election, she was at the polls early, the first woman in the state to cast a vote.

Abigail Scott Duniway died just before her eighty-first birthday. Today, it may sound extreme to call women "slaves," but in Duniway's day, when all property and rights belonged only to men, it was essentially true. Duniway changed things forever, not only in Oregon but across the United States, and she is remembered as one of our nation's leading suffragettes.

Molly Goodnight

Ranch Woman
1839–1926

Although she was born in Tennessee, Mary Ann (Molly) Dyer Goodnight was very much a woman of the American West. Praised and loved in Texas as the "Little Mother of the Panhandle," she was known for her hospitality to all, her generosity, and her love of animals. But Molly Goodnight left behind three legacies: as a ranch woman who brightened a lonely and difficult life; as the woman who saved the buffalo from extinction; and as the woman who made the sidesaddle bearable for other women of her time.

Mary Ann Dyer was born on September 12, 1839, in Madison County, Tennessee. When she was fourteen, her parents packed up the whole family—Molly and seven brothers—and moved to Texas for more room to raise their children. In less than ten years, her mother died, worn out by child-bearing and hard work. When her father died in 1864, with the older boys off fighting for the Confederacy, Molly was left to raise the younger Dyer children. Within a year or two, she lost one brother in the Civil War and another to Indian attack.

Molly taught school in Weatherford in north-central Texas, although she had never been to school herself. "My only teachers were my father and mother, both of whom were well educated for their times," she once said. "Then, too, I learned a lot from nature." She took her youngest brother with her to school each day, and they were escorted by soldiers to ward off Indian attacks.

Molly had met Texas cattleman Charles Goodnight as early as 1860, before her parents died, but she was busy raising her brothers then and he had a cattle empire to establish. It was 1870 before they married.

The newlyweds settled in Pueblo, Colorado, but the national financial panic of 1873 eventually forced Charles Goodnight to move back to Texas and go into partnership with Englishman John Adair. With his wife, Lady Cornelia, Adair accompanied the Goodnights from Colorado to the Palo Duro Canyon of the Texas Panhandle. Lady Cornelia rode horseback the entire way—sidesaddle—and Goodnight both rode and drove an ambulance. In her husband's absence, she was in charge of the cattle and cowboys. Once, looking through field glasses and mistaking a patch of bear grass for Indians, she ordered the cattle rounded up.

Lady Cornelia's was the last female companionship Goodnight would enjoy for a long time. Her comfortable log house at the Home Ranch in the canyon was 75 miles (120 km) from the nearest neighbor lady and 200 miles (322 km) from the nearest community, which was not, according to her husband, much of a community anyway, because you couldn't even buy a sunbonnet there.

To keep from being lonely, Goodnight mothered the cowhands and every wanderer who came her way. She was doctor, counselor, Sunday-school teacher, and friend. No one was turned away from her house or her table, and when Adair once objected to eating with a "servant"—one of the ranch's cowboys—it was Adair who moved and the cowboy who, reluctantly, ate at the Goodnight table. If a cowboy failed to pay attention during Sunday services, he was liable to find a gun poked in his ribs as a warning not to offend the Little Mother of the Panhandle.

Once a cowboy brought Molly three hens in a sack. "No one can ever know what a pleasure those chickens were to me, and how much company they were," she later wrote. "They would come when I called them, and they would follow me wherever I went, and I could talk to them."

At Christmas, the Goodnights entertained lavishly, and as many as 150 people came from hundreds of miles away. Long tables were loaded with roast beef, wild turkey, antelope, cakes, pies, and other delicacies. Dancing often continued until the small hours of the morning, and girls danced and rested alternately, because there were never enough girls to go around. Music was played on the fiddle, banjo, and guitar.

Perhaps because she had been separated from Charles Goodnight so much during their courtship, Molly was reluctant to have him leave her after their marriage. She often accompanied him on the trail, either driving a wagon or riding sidesaddle—no proper woman of the day would have ridden astride. Charles, realizing how uncomfortable the traditional sidesaddle was for long hours on horseback, designed a new saddle for her. It had a horn over which she could hook her left knee, rather than letting it hang unsupported. That saddle, later copied worldwide as a "safe" sidesaddle, is now part of the collection at the Panhandle-Plains Historical Museum in Canyon, Texas.

Legend has it that Colonel Goodnight (an honorary title) once roped two buffalo calves and gave them to his wife. Fascinated by the young animals, she cared for them and taught them to drink milk. Eventually, the Goodnight herd grew to 250 head, with full-grown buffalo that would take food from their owners' hands through a fence. Molly never considered it safe to walk among them on foot, but she is generally credited with saving the buffalo of the Southern Plains from extinction.

After many years in the canyon, the Goodnights settled at a railroad station nearby that was named Goodnight in their honor. Their house in Goodnight was a showplace for the time—it even had an inside bathroom and a "den" in which Colonel Goodnight could "sit and think." But there were still all kinds of enclosures for animals, including a pasture for the buffalo herd.

H
Sh
shi

set
fai
tha
ant
Lal

chi
Mc
An
Mc

and
ma
she
soo
div

aga
to
war
Wh
ene
tha
par
was

Sarah Winnemucca

Champion of Indian Rights
1844?–1891

Sarah Winnemucca was born in the mid-1840s—she thought it was 1844—in the Great Basin, now northern Nevada. Her people, the Paiute Indians, were just beginning to see white trappers and explorers come into their land. Some were afraid of the newcomers and especially of their guns. But Sarah's grandfather, Chief Truckee, believed the whites were the long-lost brothers told of in a Paiute myth. He was so glad to see these people that he even arranged for Sarah to live with a white

Some sources say that Young was afraid his other wives would be jealous of this new young wife so, instead of taking Ann Eliza to the house where most of his wives lived, he moved her into a small, shabby house. The food he had delivered was hardly worth eating, and he never sent enough money. Other sources suggest that Ann Eliza refused to live at Lion House with the other wives.

Eventually, Ann Eliza began taking her sons to Young's main residence, Lion House, for meals and prayer. The food was better than they had been getting, and though the other wives were at first suspicious of Ann Eliza, they all eventually became friends. Young continued to ignore her needs, and Ann Eliza was forced to take in boarders to survive. When her wood stove fell apart, Young refused to help. Ann Eliza sent the boarders away, sent her older son to her parents, and sought the help of a Methodist minister, Major Ponds, and his wife, with whom she had become friendly.

She decided to divorce Young and tell the world her story, but this was dangerous. At Ponds's suggestion, she and her younger son moved into a hotel where she would be safe. The Mormon Church had followers who would punish any member found speaking against the church. Ann Eliza was angry at Young, not the church, and never spoke against the church. But she was still very frightened.

When her story became known, reporters from all over began coming to Salt Lake City to talk to Ann Eliza. She received them all in her hotel room, and her name was in every newspaper. Young was furious, but he could do nothing because she was now a national figure. Major Ponds encouraged her to go on a public tour, but she was afraid to leave her hotel room. She knew the Mormons were furious with her. Finally, in disguise, she slipped out of Salt Lake City with a companion and went to Denver where she told her story to a large audience. From there, she spoke throughout the country, in spite of the lies Young told about her and the accusations he made.

At first, her mother begged her to return to the Mormon Church. But eventually even she was convinced and came to stand beside her daughter. Only then did her mother admit that plural marriage had been hard for her.

The courts did not decide the divorce matter for nearly five years. Ann Eliza received $3,600; she had asked for $200,000. But she made money from her lectures and the sale of books she wrote, including her best-known, *Wife No. 19*. Most important, she felt she had told the world about polygamy.

In 1890, the government forced the Mormon Church to give up the practice of plural marriage, although isolated instances continued well into the twentieth century. It was a sweet victory for Ann Eliza.

Her life was not all happiness though. In 1883, she married again—to a wealthy man from Michigan. However, they separated and divorced in 1893, and Ann Eliza lived alone thereafter, writing and occasionally lecturing. But the subject of polygamy was no longer of much interest to the American public, and the fame she had enjoyed disappeared. There is no record of her life after 1908.

Nellie Cashman

Restaurant Owner and Miner
1845–1925

Nellie Cashman spent more than a decade in the mining centers of Arizona and another twenty-five years in Alaska's far north. She operated restaurants and boardinghouses, took shares in other people's mines, and had her own mines. She was kind and caring, taking responsibility for raising her orphaned nieces and nephews, and making a desperate long journey to save stranded miners. But she was also tough, ambitious, and willing to go anywhere, and compete with any man where there was gold, silver, or copper to be had. She was a woman in a man's profession and working in mining camps where few proper ladies could be found. She was rough and tough, but Nellie also remained a lady.

Nellie Cashman was born in County Cork, Ireland. Like many Irish people, Nellie, her mother, and her sister Fannie came to the United States to escape the potato famine. They lived first in Boston and then in San Francisco. But Nellie was determined to make a lot of money, and things moved too slowly for her in San Francisco. When she heard of mining strikes in Nevada, Nellie knew she had found her future.

She began her mining career in 1872 at the Nevada camp called Pioche. With her mother, she opened a boardinghouse in this typical mining town—dirty and violent, with saloon brawls, fires, and fights with fists, knives, and guns. Like most mining camps, Pioche soon reached its peak and mining activity slowed down. Nellie next heard of gold in the Cassiar District of northwest British Columbia, and soon she and a group of Pioche miners left for the Cassiar District.

One of the remarkable stories of Cashman's career involves Dease Lake, where she operated a boardinghouse. By grubstaking miners—giving them food and supplies in return for a stake in their mines, she made enough money to take to a Vancouver bank in November. There she heard of disaster at Dease Lake—the miners were stranded with little food and were suffering from scurvy (a painful disease due to a diet lacking in vitamin C). Nellie wasted no time. She hired six men and packed 1,500 pounds (680 kg) of supplies, including limes to supply the needed vitamin C. They went by steamer to Fort Wrangell, then by sled for 100 miles (160 km), sometimes making only 5 miles (8 km) a day. The trip took over two months, and it was late March when the rescuers made it to Dease Lake—in time to help the miners.

Cashman stayed in British Columbia for another two years, but then thought that she might do better in Arizona. For the next twenty years she operated various businesses there—boardinghouses, hotels, and a men's store—in Tucson, Tombstone, Bisbee, and Nogales, and in Kingston, New Mexico. One of Nellie's greatest characteristics was her belief that she could succeed at whatever she did.

In Arizona she built her reputation for charitable donations and work, supporting churches and hospitals and urging others to do the same. A devout Catholic, she was always associated with the church and with Irish cultural associations.

During her years in the Southwest, Nellie's brother-in-law died. Thomas Cunningham had been a bootmaker in San Francisco, and Nellie had sold his boots in her stores. Now she brought her sister Fannie and the five young Cunninghams to Arizona and set Fannie up as manager of the Delmonico Lodging House in Tombstone. Fannie, however, suffered from tuberculosis—they called it "consumption" then—and died in 1884. Nellie was now the sole support of her elderly mother in San Francisco and her five nieces and nephews. She sent the children to various boarding schools and convents but visited them often and was in constant communication with their teachers.

Nellie had many adventures in the Southwest, including fires that wiped out entire towns. But her greatest adventure came when she decided to take a group of miners to newly discovered strikes in Baja California. The group—slightly more than twenty people—traveled by stage and train and then faced the extreme heat of the desert, where there was no water and no plants. When the journey became difficult, Nellie took five or six men and went on ahead. They came close to disaster from exhaustion and thirst. Whether they were rescued by Mexicans or their own party has never been clear, but Nellie was soon back in Arizona, rebuilding her fortune.

Some periods of her life are difficult to account for as she went rapidly from place to place in Arizona. But she was always trying to be in on the early, exciting part of a strike; when things calmed down, she moved on, seeking adventure. By the mid-1890s, she was bored with Arizona.

Newspapers then were full of the news of gold strikes in Alaska's Klondike-Yukon area so Nellie headed north in 1898. She was not the first woman to reach the Klondike. More than 1,000 women were involved in mining at that time, either as business managers or actively working the mines.

After considering several routes, Nellie chose to go from Skagway over Chilkoot Pass. The Canadian Royal Mounted Police (the Mounties) stopped everyone going in to make sure they had at least 900 pounds (400 kg) of provisions—enough to last a year. Fifty-four-year-old Nellie talked her way in and reached Dawson in April. She operated five restaurants in the area at one time or another, but probably made most of her money on mining claims. When others tried to grab her claims, she thought nothing of entering bitter legal battles.

Nellie knew that placer mining for surface deposits of minerals would soon be over in Dawson. In 1904 she left for Fairbanks, farther north, and in 1905 she went to Koyukuk River Basin, beyond the Arctic Circle. The trip was 450 miles (725 km) inland up the Yukon River by steamboat, then another 450 miles (725 km) on the Koyukuk River to St. John's-in-the-Wilderness mission at Allakaket, then 80 miles (128 km) by small craft to a trading post at Nolan Creek.

Nolan Creek was a long chapter in Nellie's life. She worked claims there for twenty years, going south or "outside"—the Alaskans term for the lower forty-eight states—several times to visit family and friends. But she always returned to Nolan Creek—a rough, inhospitable place noted for hard work, quarreling, and drinking. Nellie stayed, mining her claims, raising funds for good causes, but at seventy-six, she still said she'd pull up stakes if anything exciting appeared elsewhere.

Nellie's health gave out in 1924, on her return north from a trip to donate money for a church in Tombstone. She was hospitalized in Victoria but died on January 4, 1925. After her death, stories began to portray her as "The Miner's Angel" or "Nellie Cashman, Savior in the Wilderness." Those who knew her readily agreed that she was charitable, a steady financial and spiritual contributor to causes about which she cared. But, they remind us, she was also a stampeder, one who followed the mining rush to possible instant wealth wherever it led.

Carry Nation

Reformer
1846–1911

When people hear the name Carry Nation, they usually think of a woman dressed in black, wearing a bonnet, waving a hatchet, and breaking up saloons. Carry Nation, a reformer who fought against liquor on the frontier, earned herself the nickname of "battle-ax" by swinging a hatchet or an ax at every saloon she could find.

Carry Nation was born in Kentucky to a wandering, ne'er-do-well father and a mentally ill mother who gave her little affection and spent most of her life in an institution. At a

young age, Carry was responsible for her stepbrothers and sisters. As the old-est child in a very poor family, she had a hard time feeding and clothing the other children. A long period of illness kept her out of school and away from girls her own age. Perhaps because of her difficult childhood, Carry came to believe that she had to prove her worth in the eyes of God as she saw him.

She married a physician early, but he proved to be an alcoholic and she returned to her father's home, where she gave birth to a daughter—Charlien. Carry earned a teacher's certificate and taught school in Holden, Missouri, where she met David Nation, a lawyer, editor, and sometime minister. They were married in 1877, but she had not done much better this time in choos-ing a husband. Nation bought a farm in Texas and the family was soon hope-lessly in debt. She supported her husband and child by running a series of boardinghouses, but in 1889 they returned to Medicine Lodge, Kansas, where David Nation was minister of a small church.

Carry became a reformer in Kansas. She gave food and clothing gener-ously to the poor, but she also came to see herself as responsible for the behavior of the town. In her mind, she was proving her worth to God. To everyone else, she was "difficult." She was convinced that liquor was the world's greatest evil—it had destroyed her first husband and was now destroying her grown daughter. In 1892, Nation founded a local branch of the Woman's Christian Temperance Union (WCTU) in Kansas.

Kansas was legally dry—liquor was not supposed to be sold there—but saloons operated freely, and the law often looked the other way. Nation orga-nized women to act against the illegal bars. "The women and children . . . are calling to you men for bread, for clothes, and education," she said. She added that with men selling—and drinking—whiskey, it was no wonder the women wanted ballet and other fine entertainment.

At first, the women prayed in front of the saloons, hoping to interest the public and shame the authorities into enforcing the law. When that was not as successful as she wished, Nation began to use physical force—rocks, bricks and billiard balls—to demolish saloons. Since the bars were illegal, she reasoned that they were not protected by the law. She found the hatchet to be a most effective tool.

In 1900, she demolished a fancy bar in a Kansas hotel and was jailed for two weeks. By now, newspapers across the country were attracted by her story and carried pictures of her. She was a large, tall woman, always dressed in black with a white temperance ribbon for trim. When Nation strode into a saloon, she sang a temperance song in a loud voice.

In 1901, she was forced to give up smashing saloons and go on a lecture tour

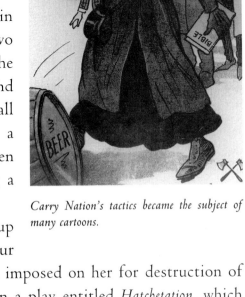

Carry Nation's tactics became the subject of many cartoons.

to earn enough money to pay the fines imposed on her for destruction of property. In 1903, she even appeared in a play entitled *Hatchetation*, which featured a scene in which she smashed a saloon with her hatchet. She was regarded as a curiosity, but the public eventually tired of her. Her husband divorced her, charging that her travels around the country to smash saloons amounted to desertion.

Carry Nation's use of violence to accomplish her ends may be seen as part of frontier thinking, where each man thought he was a law unto himself. But by the early 1900s, such thinking was clearly out of place. Carry Nation has gone down in history almost as a joke, but her name is classic among women of the American West.

Mattie Castner

Hotelkeeper, "Mother of Belt, Montana"
1848–1920

Mattie Castner was born into slavery on a North Carolina plantation. She died a wealthy landowner and a much respected citizen of Montana. In 1989, she was added to the Gallery of Outstanding Montanans in the state capitol. A plaque there reads in part, "Mattie Castner's career in Montana epitomizes the 'pioneer spirit' on which the state has been built in the twentieth century."

When Lincoln's Emancipation Proclamation of January 1, 1863, freed all slaves in the rebellious Southern states, Mattie—her last name is variously given as Bost or Bell or something similar—moved to St. Louis, Missouri, where she worked as a housekeeper, nanny, and hotel maid. In 1876, she was caring for the two children of the Sire family and when they moved to Fort Benton, Montana, Mattie followed them. She next worked as a hotel laundress, earning $100 a month—a great deal of money in those days—and then she opened her own laundry. There she met John K. Castner, a white man from Pennsylvania who hauled freight by mule train. They were married

Mattie Castner's hotel in Belt, Montana

in 1877 in Helena, Montana.

The Castners moved to a valley where John had mining claims, and he began to dig coal and haul it to Fort Benton where he sold it for $4 a ton. He and Mattie built a log cabin covered with brush, cemented with mud and buffalo chips, and lined with unbleached muslin. Soon the cabin was the center of both the growing town of Belt, Montana, and the Castner hotel. To accommodate stagecoach travelers, the Castners kept building onto their home until it sprawled in so many directions that visitors sometimes became lost in a maze of corridors.

Mattie served all the meals, including grouse, prairie chickens, deer, antelope, elk, buffalo and trout, much of which came from her own hunting expeditions. She also kept a vegetable garden and became famous for her creamed peas. A meal cost fifty cents. In addition to running the hotel, she sometimes worked in her husband's coal mines, and in summer she sold her homegrown produce in Fort Benton, driving all night to reach the town about dawn.

John Castner became involved in the mercantile business, real estate, and insurance, in addition to running his mines. In 1907, when the town of Belt was incorporated, he was elected the first mayor. Mattie, meanwhile, began to buy land. At her death, she was the single largest landowner in Belt. In spite of the recent division of the country over slavery, Mattie was well accepted by everyone she met in Montana.

Although the couple had no children of their own, the Castners adopted a baby boy abandoned at their hotel—the first white child born in Belt—and raised him to adulthood. Mattie was generous in other ways too: she donated to good causes and often delivered baskets of food to needy townspeople. Such generosity no doubt earned her the title of "Mother of Belt."

Mattie made three trips east hoping to find her parents and her five brothers and sisters. Supposedly, she located one brother, two sisters, and a niece. The rest of her family had been sold before Emancipation and she was unable to find them.

Mattie Castner retired from the hotel business in 1912. John Castner died in 1915, and Mattie in 1920. She left a large estate for that time—$25,000—and donated most of it to charity.

Pretty Shield

Crow Indian Healing Woman
1850s?—1930s?

Because the Crow Indians had no written history, little is known of the tribe's life on the Great Plains during the early and mid-nineteenth century. When historians began trying to record the history and interview tribal members, they concentrated on warriors and ignored the women. Crow women, they thought, led dull and uninteresting lives. And the Indian women themselves were so shy that interviewing them was difficult.

But Frank Bird Linderman, a

Chicagoan, went to Montana at the age of sixteen and spent the next forty years studying and writing about the Plains Indians, He interviewed the Crow healing woman Pretty Shield in the early 1930s. Reservation records indicated she was then seventy-four years old. She once said she was born in the snow when "Yellow-calf and his war party were wiped out by the Lakota [Sioux]," probably in the 1850s.

Pretty Shield did not want to talk to Linderman about reservation life when the hearts of the Crow had "turned to stone." But she told of a happy childhood and described games played by Crow children—kicking a ball made by stuffing antelope hair into the sac that surrounds a buffalo heart, and sliding down snow hillsides on a sled made of buffalo ribs.

Pretty Shield did not attend school but learned by imitating her elders, particularly a widowed aunt who raised her. She carried her doll on her back, had a miniature tepee in which she built a cooking fire. When she was seven, she was attacked by a mad buffalo bull. Trying to escape, she fell and drove a stick into her forehead and against one eye. She did not lose her sight but carried the scar of that encounter for the rest of her life. When she was fourteen, Pretty Shield and a group of other girls were treed by a grizzly bear and her cubs. All her life, Pretty Shield remembered looking down into the eyes of the grizzly and smelling the bears, a smell that made her sick.

At sixteen, she became the second wife of Goes Ahead, whose first wife was Pretty Shield's older sister. She gave birth to four girls and three boys, but one girl and one boy died as infants. While grieving over their deaths, she had the vision that led her to become a healer.

When Crow women grieved, they cut their hair short and slashed their arms, legs, and face to show their suffering. Then they wandered without food or water until their grief became less intense. During this period, Pretty Shield saw a woman who led her to an anthill and told her to first rake the edges of the anthill and then ask for anything she wanted. Pretty Shield asked for "good luck and a good life." After that, the ants—"busy, powerful little people"—were her medicine.

Pretty Shield treated the illnesses of Crow women and children, mostly using medicinal plants and often acting as a counselor. She did not charge a fee, but was paid in gifts—tobacco, elks' teeth, buffalo robes, and food.

Talking to Linderman, Pretty Shield was sad when she described the disappearance of the traditional Crow way of life. The Crow believed they would follow the buffalo herds on the plains forever, as they had done for centuries. Instead, the hide hunters came—men who killed buffalo for their hides and left the carcasses to rot on the plains. Pretty Shield's beloved plains smelled of rotting meat, and now the buffalo herds had disappeared.

"I am walking in the dark," she told Linderman. "Ours was a different world before the buffalo went away, and I belong to that other world."

Pretty Shield's words to Linderman provided a clear picture of the traditional life of the tribe. In this way, she helped preserve the Crow heritage for later generations.

Women on the Stage

Women were few and hard to find in the West for much of the nineteenth century, and their company was in great demand by men. Because they had so few women in their daily lives, Western men became enthusiastic theatergoers whenever a woman was performing. One woman's presence on a stage could be shared by a whole audience of men. At that time, there were five times as many actresses for the population in the West as in the East, and many women gained fame on frontier stages.

Frontier men went to the theater just to see the women. But though they were enthusiastic, Western men were not always uncritical. Rowdy male audiences out West demanded entertainment—they wanted a rollicking good time, and they loved the spectacular. They did not tolerate poor performances, sometimes tossing the offending actress in a blanket and ushering her out of town.

Once, when an overage, overweight actress sang poorly, a man in the audience suggested they take up a collection so she could retire early. The actress was then pelted with silver coins.

Lola Montez was recognized as one of the beauties of the age.

Lotta Crabtree became a very successful actress on the Western stage.

Lola Montez (1818-1861) was probably the most talked-about stage performer of the West in her time. In spite of her Spanish-sounding name, Lola was Irish by birth. After a difficult childhood in India and England and an early, unfortunate marriage, she went to Spain to learn Spanish dancing. Her English debut, however, was ruined when someone in the audience recognized her as Betty James. Thereafter, she roamed Europe, performing as an actress and gaining international fame and recognition as one of the beauties of the age.

In the 1850s, a scandal drove her to America, where she was greeted as a heroine. Deciding to try her luck out West, she headed for San Francisco where tickets to her first performance sold for $65, an enormous sum in those days.

Lola left a legacy of sorts in the form of a young actress named Lotta Crabtree. Lotta was a young child in Grass Valley, California, when Lola Montez retired to that community. Lola taught Lotta to ride, dance, and sing. With red hair in long curls, flashing black eyes, and a voice full of laughter, Lotta debuted on the public stage at the age of eight, doing an Irish jig. The miners loved her.

By the time she was in her teens, in the 1860s, Lotta was baring her legs and smoking on stage. It was not "ladylike," but Lotta got away with it because her admirers were convinced it was all done in a spirit of childish innocence. Lotta emphasized this image by finishing each performance clad in white, singing a tear-jerking ballad. Proper ladies adored her as much as the miners did.

Serious drama was less popular in the West than the eye-catching spectacles offered by Lola, Lotta, and others like them. In 1881, the famed English actress Sarah Bernhardt appeared in *Camille* in St. Joseph, Missouri. One critic complained that she was "distressingly ugly . . . with arms as long and wiry as the tendrils of devil-fish."

As the West grew more civilized, its citizens' taste in theater grew more formal. By 1890, neither Lola nor Lotta would have been tolerated by theatergoers who looked forward to an evening in the theater as a proper social occasion and expected to be rewarded with serious offerings. The rough miners who cheered and stamped their approval were replaced by well-dressed men and women who clapped politely.

Mary Hallock Foote

Author and Illustrator
1847–1938

Mary Hallock Foote left twelve novels and numerous stories, articles, and sketches, all of which attempt to capture the American West as she saw it and as she believed other Easterners saw it. Foote followed her mining-engineer husband to California, Idaho, and Mexico and lived in the American West for more than fifty years.

Born in 1847 in Milton, New York, and raised a Quaker, Mary attended Cooper Union Institute School of Design in New York City where she showed a talent for illustration. Soon she was doing illustrations for *Harper's Weekly,* a leading magazine of the day, and even illustrating Henry Wadsworth Longfellow, Nathaniel Hawthorne, and Lord Alfred Tennyson. She met and knew famous authors and writers of the day and lived a sophisticated city life.

Then she met Arthur Foote, an engineer who had just returned from the American West, a man whose whole life and being stood in sharp contrast to the city life she knew. They were married in 1876, and, although Foote was reluctant to leave her artistic life, she followed her husband to California that summer.

Having discovered she could still read, write, and draw in what she saw as the wilderness, she began to write long letters to friends back home, describing the countryside and people around her. Richard Watson Gilder, editor of the important magazine *Scribner's* and later of *The Century,* asked Foote to turn her letters into articles.

She began with "A California Mining Camp," which was based on her life at New Almaden, and "A Sea-Port on the Pacific," describing the city of Santa Cruz where she waited while Arthur tried to find a new job. Her first child, Arthur Burlington Foote, was born in 1877. Mary Hallock Foote followed her husband to Leadville, Colorado, and the Michoacán province of Mexico in the next years, often leaving her son with her family in Milton. Two more children—daughters Betty and Agnes—were born to the couple, although Agnes died in 1904.

From 1883 to 1895 the family lived in Idaho where Arthur worked on irrigation projects. Next came Grass Valley, California, where Arthur managed the North Star Mine until his retirement in 1914, when young Arthur took over as manager. The Footes lived in retirement in Grass Valley, until moving back east in 1932. Mary Hallock Foote died in 1938 at the age of ninety-one.

Foote is probably best known today for the novel, *The Led-Horse Claim,* a love story set against the background of a conflict over rights to mining property. She is also remembered for her memoir, *A Victorian Gentlewoman in the Far West.* In that and other novels, Foote presented frontier life realistically, especially the difficulties that faced a woman from the East. She brought a woman's point of view to the conflict between Eastern and Western ways. Mary Hallock Foote's life inspired Wallace Stegner's classic novel, *Angle of Repose.*

The Army Women

1865–1876

After the Civil War, the U.S. Cavalry went west to conquer the American Indian tribes west of the Mississippi River who had roamed freely there for centuries. Two types of women followed them.

The lesser-known women were laundresses—the only women officially recognized as part of a garrison. The row of houses they lived in was known as Soapsuds Row. The women received housing, food, fuel, payment, and other benefits from the army—but they worked hard for them. They washed soldiers' uniforms by hand, using a washboard, and ironed them with a sad-iron (an iron that had to be heated on the stove frequently, as it quickly lost its heat). Many laundresses were married to enlisted men, but they earned more than their husbands. Most of them were good, hard working, honest women. The few who were not have given a shady name to Soapsuds Row.

At the other end of the social scale were the officers' wives. In a different way, their lives were equally difficult. They were moved from post to post so often that they barely had time to settle in one place before they had to pack again. They often went from the comfort of an Eastern post to the searing desolation of a post like Fort Yuma in the Arizona desert or the bitter cold of a Montana winter.

Housing for officers generally ranged from barely acceptable to awful, and many officers' wives lived in places that would have made a settler's sod hut look like a palace. Quarters were often insect-infested cottonwood-log cabins with dirt floors, or drafty wooden houses through which the winter winds whistled. When a new officer came to a post, he could choose his living quarters by "ranking out" anyone beneath him. The officer who was ranked out would then rank out someone beneath him, and the process went through the fort like falling dominoes.

Life was hard for these women, especially when they waited for the return of husbands out on patrol. But there were benefits, including a fairly active social life. At any post there might be games, band concerts, card parties, amateur theatricals, sewing bees, skating, sleighing in winter, lawn tennis in warmer weather, croquet, hunting for prairie chickens and grouse, and long rides on the prairie.

Army wives were always thought to be in great danger from Indians, although after 1861 there is not one recorded instance of a woman killed at an army post by Indians. They were actually in more danger from their overprotective husbands. Major General George Armstrong Custer made it plain to his officers that the person in charge of his wife's safety was to shoot her in case of attack. Once Elizabeth (Libbie) Custer was with a detachment of 50 men during an attack by 600 Indians. After a three-hour battle, the Indians withdrew, but the colonel in charge told Libbie he had been preparing to shoot her. "Would you have given me no chance for life in case the battle had not gone in your favor?" she asked. "Not one," he replied.

Mrs. Custer left the best record of life as an army officer's wife during that period in her books, *Tenting on the Plains, Boots and Saddles,* and *Following the Guidon.* She recorded beauty where most would have seen none, writing that a "rare exultant feeling takes possession of one in the gallops over the Plains" and guessing that "the sky fits close down all around" surely was said of the plains. Still, she also wrote of dreary trips over boring country only to end in a small post of log cabins. And she described Kansas as "hot, blistered earth, dry beds of streams, and soil apparently so barren that not even the wildflowers would bloom . . . add pestilence, Indians, and an undisciplined muti- nous soldier. . . ."

Like that of most army wives, life for Libbie was full of ter-

George Custer and his wife, Libbie, shared many adventures in the West.

rors, both real and imaginary. New to the plains, she lived through a prairie storm, describing herself as "quaking and terrified under the covers . . . alone in a tent, a kind of 'rag house' which might have been a handkerchief."

There were Indians to worry about, too. Once Libbie and a young officer walked out of quarters at dusk. They were mistaken for Indians in the near-darkness and shot at by sentries. The officer ordered Libbie to lie flat in the grass to avoid being fired upon while he crept back to the post. For Libbie, the terror of being left alone in the darkness was almost worse than being shot at.

The worst ordeal, however, was the anxiety. Any vision of dashing troopers in colorful uniforms faded before the reality of men marching out on an Indian campaign. Following her husband's departure, there were "days of anxiety, and nights of hideous dreams of what might befall him." When he once returned unexpectedly, she wrote, "There was in that summer of 1867 one long, perfect day. It was mine, and—blessed by our memory . . . it is still mine, for time and for eternity."

Libbie Custer's days on the frontier ended as they did for too many army wives—with the death of her husband. The Battle of the Little Bighorn, known among the Plains Indians as the Battle of Greasy Grass and by Americans at the time as Custer's Last Stand, was the last major victory for the Plains Indians. It demonstrated the Indians' determination to defend their land and their way of life.

Libbie was a widow for fifty-six long years, and she spent those years building up her husband's reputation as a hero. No one would come forward to contradict Libbie while she lived, and many who knew the truth of the Battle of the Little Bighorn died before she did. As a result, Custer was considered the martyr-hero of that battle for many years. Today, we know that he foolishly led his men into a position they could not defend.

Libbie was made of stern stuff though. When word was brought to her of Custer's death, she threw a wrap over her dressing gown and accompanied the captain to the twenty-five other widows of that battle to offer them consolation.

Georgia Arbuckle Fix

Physician
1852–1918

It was the kind of accident that happened too often on pioneer homesteads in western Nebraska. Eli Beebe had been helping dig a new well, using a windlass—a type of winch—and bucket to hoist the dirt out as he dug. As Beebe slowly cranked another bucket to the top, his hand slipped from the windlass, and the heavy load of dirt crashed to the bottom of the well. The whirling windlass struck him in the head, tearing out a chunk of his skull.

Word of the accident was sent to Dr. Georgia Arbuckle, but her cabin was across the prairie, a long hard ride away. Dr. Arbuckle threw on her cowhide coat, grabbed her medical kit, and started across the prairie. When she reached Beebe, he was unconscious with part of his brain exposed by the hole in his skull. Dr. Arbuckle cleaned the wound and wondered how to cover it. Taking a silver dollar from her purse, she asked for a hammer. The dollar was pounded flat, sterilized, and sewn into Beebe's head—the first successful use of silver plate in brain surgery. It is said that Eli Beebe rode in a rodeo parade at the age of seventy-something, the silver dollar still in his head.

Georgia Arbuckle had worked hard to become a doctor. She was born in Princeton, Missouri, to a single mother. When she was about nine, her mother married and moved west for her health. Young Georgia stayed behind with Dr. Dinsmore and his family, who gave her not only a home but books to read. Soon she was reading medical texts. When Dr. Dinsmore moved to the State University of Omaha's College of Medicine in Nebraska, Georgia followed. She was the only woman in the class of 1883, and her classmates often played practical jokes on her to show that they did not think a woman belonged in medical school. She worked her way through school doing nursing, cleaning, whatever she could. After graduation, she practiced medicine briefly in Omaha and was an officer in the Douglas County Medical Society, an unusual honor for a woman at that time.

Meantime, Georgia's stepfather and half-brother had moved to western Nebraska, and in 1886 she followed them. They built her a sod house at the only place on the North Platte River where there were three trees. (The town of Minatare is located near there today.)

Georgia Arbuckle became a familiar figure in western Nebraska, riding alone across the prairie, sometimes on horseback, sometimes in a buggy, always wearing her cowhide coat and carrying her medical bag. She learned to "read" the prairie—watching for cattle trails, rises in the land, buffalo wallows, anything that would help her find her way back home through that sea of grass. Like many pioneer women, she had a strong sense of direction that kept her from getting lost. In later years, she drove in a buggy with a horse that seemed to know where it was going. Once she was called to see a sick baby. Years later, a woman staying with the baby's family said, "I can see her yet, raising up and groping back to consciousness when the team stopped. Her hair was long and black and straight. During the drive it had fallen down. She sat up and began pinning it into place in a coil on top of her head. Then she got out of the buggy, brushed her clothes, and was ready for work."

She set broken legs and arms for cowboys, delivered babies for women in lonely farmhouses, pulled teeth when she had to, and even spoke over new graves when there was no preacher. Once, in the middle of the night, a cowboy with an unbearable toothache asked her to pull his tooth. She told him to sit in a chair and grab both arms tightly while his friend held his head. But when she began to pull the tooth, the cowboy slowly drew his feet up. Heavy spurs raked across the floor—and then across the doctor's foot. "Careful!" she shouted. "I'm no bronc!"

In 1888, she met a young man named Gwynn Fix, who was known for driving a fast team of horses—but not for holding a job. The two were married, but it was not a happy marriage. Their most serious differences were over money. Dr. Fix was often paid in kind—she received chickens, eggs, wild fruit, butter, whatever the family could offer in return for her services. Over the years she had received several cattle in payment, and she had built up a nice herd. Her husband sold the cattle without her permission.

In 1909 she filed for divorce from Mr. Fix—a bold thing for a woman to do in those days—and when her neighbors gossiped about her, she wrote in her journal, "You cannot sew buttons on your neighbor's mouth."

Dr. Fix moved to the nearby town of Gering, where she remodeled a two-story house into a hospital. It became known as "The Sanitarium."

Surrounded by trees and filled with dogs and birds—as well as patients—it was a favorite place for the children of Gering, and young girls often boarded there while they studied in town. The sanitarium then became the site of several weddings. Dr. Fix was also active in her community: the women's exchange, organized to raise funds for village improvements, began in the sanitarium, as did the women's library club and the women's missionary society.

Georgia Arbuckle Fix retired from her medical practice in 1916 and moved to California, worn out by long hours and long trips across the prairie to see her patients. She died in 1918 at the age of sixty-six, but she is remembered as the first woman doctor in Nebraska.

The story of Georgia Arbuckle Fix has been told in the novel *Miss Morissa* by Mari Sandoz and *Mattie* by Judy Alter.

May Arkwright Hutton

Mining Camp Cook and Millionaire Suffragette
1860–1915

right to vote

May Arkwright Hutton used to say that she wouldn't trade the whole of Ohio for the Idaho panhandle. She was raised—or raised herself—in Ohio. Her mother disappeared early in her life, and her wandering father didn't want the responsibility of a young child. He turned her over to her blind grandfather. She led the old man around town, listened to him talk, and once went with him to hear future President William McKinley speak. She would later trace several characteristics back to this strange childhood—a strong interest in the daily news, a better understanding of men than of women, and a wish to reform the world.

May was a large woman—big-boned and weighing some 200 pounds (90 kg). In 1883, twenty-three years old and widowed after a brief and unhappy marriage, she decided to take off for Idaho where she knew mining camps needed cooks. But she didn't go alone. She talked forty young Ohio coal miners into going with her to search for gold. It never bothered May that it was hardly proper for a woman to travel alone with forty men!

In Idaho, she went into the restaurant business in a mining area called Eagle City, in the Coeur d'Alene area. She worked hard and saved her money, using it to buy interests (percentages) in miners' holes. She was determined to get rich. The other women in the mining camps were pretty and painted while May was big and homely, but the men liked her—they called her Mame—and they enjoyed her cooking. In 1885, a major outcropping was discovered in nearby Wardner Junction, and May moved her restaurant business there. She bought a cow, a broom, a bucket, a cookstove, a piece of land, and a two-room shack.

May knew that most miners failed because they could not wait for work to bring them wealth. They moved from claim to claim and from job to job. She also believed that mine owners took advantage of them and that a union was the only thing that would help the miners. She also believed passionately in women's right to vote and in equal rights, and she spoke out for the housewife, the old-maid schoolteacher, the overworked mother, and the miner's widow.

In 1887, a new railroad engineer walked into May's restaurant. He was Levi W. (Al) Hutton. They shared memories of orphaned and unhappy childhoods, and Al came to see her as his future wife. She was fat, but she had a powerful personality; he was self-confident enough that he was not afraid of being run over by her. They were married within weeks after meeting, in a formal ceremony with invitations, a minister, a bridesmaid—and lots of May's home-cooked food. May wore a gown of light blue plush—and a large bustle.

When Al was transferred 12 miles (19 km) north to the town of Wallace, they bought a two-room shack on a mountainside, and May took over supervision of the dining room at the Wallace Hotel. When labor disputes hit the area and a mill was blown up, May was right in the middle of the action, listening to the talk, sympathizing with the miners. She lived through the quarrels, feuds, and murders of the "Rocky Mountain Revolution," the troubles of 1892, and the even greater troubles of 1899 when trains were taken over—including one engineered by Al—and one of the largest mills in North America was blown to bits.

When Al was arrested and imprisoned with other miners in a crude stockade, May visited the stockade daily and just as often wrote letters to the editor of the *Spokane Review,* expressing in strong language her anger at the mine owners who opposed labor unions. Somewhere along the way she decided to turn the story into a novel, *The Coeur d'Alene or a Tale of the Modern Inquisition in Idaho.* The book, now a collector's item, combines a sentimental love affair with the labor disputes and condemns mine owners with exaggerated accusations. Some threatened to sue, but it would have been useless—the Huttons had no money.

It wasn't too long, though, before they were rich. In the late 1880s, when two longtime friends accidentally discovered a rich lode of galena (the principal ore or mineral of lead), the couple immediately bought shares of the claim—the Hercules. For twelve years, it was almost a joke, but in 1901, the Hercules revealed the richest silver ore ever found in that area.

For May, the road to wealth and influence had been long but determined. She had left Ohio, moved from mining camp to mining camp, married Al Hutton, moved to Wallace, invested in the Hercules, and written her book, all with her goal in mind. Now, in her forties, she had reached success. The

Huttons bought a two-story home on flat land (not in the mountains!), and May began entertaining—lodge groups, union communities, county Democrats, high school graduating classes. Soon she was inviting celebrities and national leaders to her home—and they were accepting. Clarence Darrow, the famous lawyer, dined with her, and so did poet Ella Wheeler Wilcox, suffragette Carrie Chapman Catt, and even President Theodore Roosevelt. She dressed outrageously, joined the Shakespeare Club, traveled to Mexico and back to Ohio, and saw her name in the Spokane newspaper for having given a banquet in honor of suffragette Susan B. Anthony. Nominated by the Democratic Party for the state legislature, she lost to a Republican and told reporters, "What do you expect with $20,000 spent underground to defeat me?"

In 1907, the Huttons moved to the city of Spokane, where they had many friends and where investment and business opportunities were more plentiful than in Wallace. They built a downtown office building, the Hutton Block, and lived in an apartment on the top floor. May went in search of projects and soon was on the board of a small home for orphans. Then she became active in the Florence Crittendon home for unwed mothers and actively worked to find solid, hard working ranchers as husbands for these girls. She was on the mayor's Charity Commission, fought for new city government and jail reform, denied that wealth had softened her sympathy for the poor, owned a box at the theater, and continued to dress outrageously, with a special fondness for plumes and feathers. Spokane never knew whether to laugh at her or with her.

Women's suffrage was still her most important cause, but May met defeat here. Her loud voice and brazen manner offended other suffragettes who thought dignity important to their movement, and May was snubbed. Her reaction? "My name hasn't spelled defeat yet, and I propose to continue to have it spell success in the future . . . ."

In 1912 she was a delegate to the state Democratic convention and then to the national Democratic convention. Friends from the early suffragette days wrote a poem to honor her:

The people all 'o this here town,
    They gotta quit kickin' our gal aroun'.
We don't care if she isn't thin;
    The suffrage fight she sure did win.

The convention was a triumph, but it took a heavy toll on May's health. The weather was unusually hot, which was hard on Hutton, and after the convention, she insisted on touring Ohio to speak for suffrage. She returned home in poor health and never quite recovered.

Although she still took up causes—avoiding U. S. involvement in World War I was one of them—she no longer had the enthusiasm she once showed. May Arkwright Hutton died at the age of fifty-five, her huge body worn out not only by her weight but by the energy she poured into everything she did.

Al Hutton lived another thirteen years, and the great interest of his last years was building the Hutton Settlement, a home for orphaned children that consisted of small cottages, each with its own housemother, rather than one large institutional building. "I want individualism . . . to get away from the uniform idea of most orphanages where every child is molded in the same pattern." Al Hutton had learned a lot from living with May.

The Outlaws

1860–1900

Inevitably, there were women in the Old West who rode the outlaw trail. Some people have suggested that the rough life of the Old West—no law and order, no refined society—turned these women into outlaws.

A long list could be put together—Cattle Kate, Rose of the Cimarron, Cattle Annie, Little Britches, Pearl Hart—but two of the most notorious were Belle Starr and Calamity Jane. Belle Starr spent one stretch in jail and was generally considered to be a horse and cattle thief. Calamity Jane was less likely an outlaw than simply an outrageous eccentric, but because of her rough and rowdy nature, she is generally classed with the female "bad guys" of the West.

Belle Starr (1848–1889) was born Myra Maybelle Shirley in northwestern Arkansas. Beyond that one fact about her life, it is difficult to separate folklore from fact. Legend has it that she was from a family of aristocratic Virginians who had settled in Missouri and who rode with the infamous Southern guerrilla Quantrill on his raids against Union, or Northern, sympathizers. One of her brothers did ride with Quantrill, and legend says that Belle strapped on a pistol too, at least once. When her brother was killed by

Yankees during the Civil War, the family moved to Texas. There Belle met up with the former Quantrill raiders—only now they were outlaws, robbing banks and railroad trains.

In every story about her, Belle's name is linked with the famous outlaw Cole Younger, but the link is uncertain and Younger denied it. Still, he is often suggested as the father of her daughter, Pearl. Belle was, however, married to Jim Reed, who also had outlaw ways and was killed in 1874.

Belle next married Sam Starr, who was three-quarters Cherokee and also an outlaw. They lived in Oklahoma where their home was a hideout for outlaws. Sam gets credit for Belle's only arrest—with him, she was accused of stealing horses and sentenced by the famous "Hanging Judge"

Belle Starr

and Indians and long for the days of glory and adventure (actually, they almost never fought one another and cowboy life was monotonous beyond belief!). But as a nation, we continue to believe that there is something different, something more grand and free about the American West as opposed to the East, which is bound up in old and now meaningless rules and habits.

Is it true? Is there still a difference about women of the American West? Probably so.

For one thing, in spite of cities such as Houston, Los Angeles, Tucson, Las Vegas and others, the West is a land of open space. If you think it has been settled or, to use Turner's term—the frontier has been closed—fly from east to west sometime and look down at the vast expanses of open land. Something different is born in the spirit of those who live in that wide space—a friendly openness, for one thing, a knowledge that it is important to know and trust your neighbor, a sense of community.

And the West is still a land of extremes of geography and climate. With blinding snowstorms, tornadoes that rip through whole towns, hailstones as large as tennis balls, grasshopper plagues that destroy a season's crops, the American West to this day is not a place for the timid, particularly not in its rural areas.

And then there is the heritage of the West—the shaping of a person's life by the myth of the American West. If you live in the land of John Wayne heroes and brave settlers who fought off Indians, and the land where Sam Houston won freedom for Texas by conquering an overpowering number of Mexican troops, there's an ideal to live up to. Not everyone in the West feels the importance of this legacy, of course, but many do.

And women? Most of us in the American West know that it took tough, strong women to settle and survive here, to enjoy the adventure of those golden years. Today, in the settled twentieth century, are we going to be any less? Of course not.

That's why we still have extraordinary women of the West today—astronauts, Olympic athletes, politicians and congresswomen, artists and journalists. The women of the American West—whether born there or immigrants—are still extraordinary.

The Ingalls Wilder Women

It is impossible to tell the story of Laura Ingalls Wilder (1867–1957), author of the "Little House on the Prairie" books, without telling the stories of her mother and daughter. Caroline Quiner Ingalls, Laura's mother, was a pioneer homesteader who followed her husband from Wisconsin to Kansas, Minnesota, and the Dakota Territory. Laura Ingalls Wilder was a farmer, an early advocate of women's rights, a writer, and, in her sixties, a novelist. Her daughter, Rose Wilder Lane, was a journalist and prolific author who encouraged Laura to write and publish the "Little House" series.

Caroline Quiner was raised in Milwaukee County, Wisconsin, one of seven children in a family of Scottish ancestry. Laura later wrote that her mother's Scottish thrift helped the family survive during hard times. Although raised on the frontier, she was a well-educated, gentle, and proud woman. When her father died, neighboring Indians brought the family food in the winter.

In 1860, Caroline married Charles Ingalls and they moved to northwestern Wisconsin, building their first homestead near Lake Pepin. While living

Laura Ingalls Wilder

in the "big woods," Caroline gave birth to two daughters, Mary and Laura. The family then moved to Montgomery County, Kansas, where Carrie was born. The area was still part of the Indian territory, and the Indians were upset at the number of white settlers moving in. One day they surrounded the Ingalls' cabin, but Caroline, possibly remembering the Indians who had fed her as a child, came out of the house to give them fresh bread. The Ingalls family was left unharmed.

Next, the family moved to Plum Creek, near Walnut Grove, Minnesota. Here the only son, Charles Frederick, was born and died. They lived two years in Iowa, where Grace was born in 1877, but returned to Walnut Grove. In 1879, the four daughters contracted scarlet fever. Mary, trying to help her mother, got out of bed too soon, had a relapse, and became permanently blind.

In the summer of 1879, the family moved to DeSmet in the Dakota Territory. After Charles (or "Pa") died in 1902, Caroline lived in the De-Smet home with Mary and Carrie and devoted herself to caring for her blind daughter. Mary had attended the Iowa State College for the Blind but was unable to be a schoolteacher as she dreamed. She returned to the family home and never married.

Caroline died in 1924 at the age of eighty-three and Mary died in 1928 of a stroke. Some say she never recovered from the loss of her mother.

The other Ingalls sisters went on to live full and interesting lives. Carrie became a printer and worked on newspapers in Colorado and South Dakota before marrying David Swanzey. Grace, the family's baby, married Nathan Dow. They farmed in several locations, then returned to DeSmet where Grace wrote for the local newspaper.

It remained for Laura to tell the family's story. She had begun teaching school at fifteen, in order to help pay Mary's tuition at the school for the blind. In 1895 she married Almanzo (Manley) Wilder, a homesteader. It is said that Laura objected to the word "obey" in the marriage vows and that Manley agreed. Theirs was an equal partnership.

Life in the little grey house on their Dakota tree claim (one of the few pieces of land with trees on it) began with a series of tragedies for the young couple. Their house burned only days after the death of their infant son, and a $3,000 wheat crop was ruined by hail. When both young parents became sick with diphtheria, they sent their daughter, Rose, to DeSmet to live with Caroline. Manley's recovery was slow, complicated by a stroke, and Laura learned to do all kinds of farmwork with machinery—riding the binder and driving a six-horse team.

In 1894, with Rose home again, the Wilders moved to Mansfield, Missouri, and made a $100 partial payment on 40 acres (16 hectares) in the Ozark Mountains. Laura and Manley built a one-room log cabin with a rock fireplace, cleared the land and planted a garden. With the help of neighbors, they built a barn for the horses and a chicken shed. Eventually, "Rocky Ridge Farm" had 200 acres (81 hectares) of improved land, plus a herd of cows, good hogs, and the "best flock of laying hens in the country."

Laura began to write—a newspaper column, essays, and articles for St. Louis newspapers, *The Country Gentleman, McCall's, Youth Companion,* and other magazines. She was sixty-five in 1932 when she wrote her first novel, *Little House in the Big Woods.* The other books in the series are *Farmer Boy* (1933); *Little House on the Prairie* (1935); *On the Banks of Plum Creek* (1937); *By the Shores of Silver Lake* (1939); *The Long Winter* (1940); *Little Town on the Prairie* (1941); and *These Happy Golden Years* (1943). Together, the books are a social history of westward movement in this country from 1870 to 1890. They grew directly out of Laura's memories of her childhood and are so totally based on fact that not even the names of the people were changed. She once said, "I lived everything that happened in my books. . . . Running through all the stories like a golden thread is the same thought of values . . . . courage, self-reliance, independence, integrity, and helpfulness."

Laura Ingalls Wilder lived to see her books become popular. She died in 1957 at the age of ninety.

Without Rose Wilder Lane, the Ingalls-Wilder family story might well have remained obscure. A bright but restless young student, Rose left her parents home in 1904 at seventeen to work as a Western Union telegraph operator and took part in the first Western Union strike for better employment conditions. In 1909, she moved to San Francisco, where she was a real-estate agent for three years.

In 1914, she began yet another career as a reporter and feature writer for the *San Francisco Bulletin.* She was writing articles about famous movie stars when her mother came to visit. Laura wrote home to Manley, "The more I see of how Rose works, the better satisfied I am to raise chickens. . . . I could not be driven by the work as she is for anything."

Rose had married Gillette Lane in 1909, but in 1918 she divorced him and began working for the Red Cross, traveling in Iraq, Turkey, and Europe until 1921. She visited many countries whose customs were far different from those of her childhood and out of these adventures she wrote *The Peaks of Shala* (1922).

Rose wrote constantly, turning out books of fiction and nonfiction along with short stories and articles. Her short story, "Innocence," won the 1922 O. Henry Prize and other stories appeared in *The Saturday Evening Post, Ladies' Home Journal, Redbook,* and other leading magazines of the day. Among her books are *Henry Ford's Own Story, The Making of Herbert Hoover, Give Me Liberty,* and *The Women's Day Book of Needlework.*

From 1943 to 1945, Rose was book review editor for the National Economic Council, and in 1965 she traveled to Vietnam where she was a correspondent for *Women's Day.* Rose did not like the politics of the country at that time, and she retired to a farm in Danbury, Connecticut, at the age of fifty-five. She died in 1968.

Rose Wilder Lane might never have traveled to Iraq, Albania, and Vietnam without the courage she inherited from Caroline Quiner Ingalls. And without Rose Wilder Lane, we might never have Laura Ingalls Wilder's picture of frontier life. It was Lane who encouraged her mother to turn her memoirs into stories. Lane then rewrote the stories to such an extent that she is considered a co-author by some. Lane also saw the books through the publication process, though her mother took credit as author. The lives and writing of the three women combined to bring us the "Little House" books treasured by so many readers of all ages.

Annie Oakley

Shootist and Wild West Show Star
1860–1926

Probably no one woman in the last century is more a part of the American West than Annie Oakley, but the truth is that she was only west of the Mississippi River once or twice and then not until she was well along in her career with Buffalo Bill's Wild West Show. Today, in part due to the stage show *Annie, Get Your Gun!* the name of Annie Oakley is familiar to millions of Americans, most of whom think she was a Westerner—as she was in spirit, if not in fact.

Born Phoebe Anne Moses, she

grew up in the woods of western Ohio, one of seven children born to a frequently widowed mother. The colorful legend is that she took her father's shotgun and taught herself to shoot so that she could put rabbit, squirrel, and game birds on her family's table. One day she appeared in the nearby town with a string of grouse and quail, which she sold to the general store. Soon she was selling her game birds to the local hotel, where she was particularly appreciated because her birds were always head-shot. ("Head-shot" means that she shot the birds cleanly through the head and did not scatter birdshot through the edible portions of the bird, thereby sparing diners from having to pick shot out of their meat as they ate.) Whatever the truth, she was an exceptionally sure shot at a young age.

As a young woman, with no skills except sharpshooting—at eleven she could neither read nor write—she moved to Cincinnati to live with a sister and brother-in-law. There, having always disliked her name and insisted on being called Annie rather than Phoebe Ann, she took the last name of Oakley. It was apparently the name of a suburb or wooded area outside the city.

In Cincinnati she competed in an exhibition match sponsored by the local German Shooting Club. The members were so impressed they arranged a match with the best marksman they knew—a man named Frank Butler, who made his living teaching and giving shooting exhibitions. Thinking he was matched against a young girl who couldn't possibly outshoot him, Butler was surprised to lose 26–25. He was also surprised to fall in love, and Oakley and Butler were married on June 22, 1876. She was sixteen and he was twenty-six. They toured together, giving shows, and Butler taught his young wife to read and write. They performed briefly with the Sells Brothers Circus and in 1885 found themselves abandoned in New Orleans when the show closed. Buffalo Bill's show was also in New Orleans, so they hired on with him, though he was at first reluctant to hire a woman sharpshooter. However, hoping to bring new excitement to his show, he took Annie on trial—and immediately hired her when he saw what she could do with a rifle or a shotgun. Butler withdrew from competition to promote his wife's career.

Annie Oakley became, next to Buffalo Bill himself, the greatest of the Wild West stars. She was called "America's Sweetheart" by the newspapers, "Little Sure Shot" by Sitting Bull, the Sioux chief Buffalo Bill had hired for the show, and "Missie" by Buffalo Bill himself. In a show filled with cowboys and Indians, she was the only white woman, and she was billed as a "Little Girl of the Western Plains." No one knew she had never set foot in the West.

Annie Oakley usually had the second spot on the program. Supposedly, she was to get the women in the audience used to gunfire early in the program, preparing them for the noisy demonstrations by Cody and others. Apparently, gunfire was thought less likely to offend if a woman did the shooting.

Annie was prim, proper, and tiny—barely 5 feet (152 cm) tall. Almost childlike, she charmed audiences as she skipped onto the stage. But she could shoot—clay pigeons, playing cards, 943 out of 1,000 glass balls, 4,772 rifle shots out of 5,000 in nine hours. Her most famous trick was splitting a playing card edgewise, but sometimes Butler held a card and she shot holes through the spots—hearts, clubs, spades or diamonds. Tickets with holes punched in them became known as "Annie Oakleys" because of these cards.

The first recorded mention of Annie riding a horse was in 1886, when she rode into the ring wearing a deerskin jacket and fringed skirt and shot from horseback. Never mind that in the movie, *Annie, Get Your Gun!* she performs extraordinary tricks on horseback—she was not a horsewoman! In 1887, the show toured Europe and played for the 50th-anniversary celebration of England's Queen Victoria as well as for Emperor Wilhelm I of Germany, who insisted Oakley shoot a cigarette from his mouth. Europeans were fascinated with Wild West shows because they assumed they represented everyday life in the American West.

With Buffalo Bill, Oakley played the World's Columbian Exposition in 1893 and, in 1896, she made her first trip west. The show went to North Platte, Nebraska, Buffalo Bill's hometown where he had staged his first show in 1876. Until the late 1890s, there were no cities in the West big enough to make it worthwhile for the show to travel there.

In 1901, the train the show traveled on was in a wreck. More than 100 horses were killed, and Oakley was injured; she never again worked for Buffalo Bill. Oakley and Butler retired to Pinehurst, North Carolina, where they taught shooting and put on exhibitions for a tourist hotel. There in 1917 she learned of the death of Buffalo Bill. By then, his show had failed, and the national interest in Wild West shows was over.

By the time Oakley was in her sixties, her own health was failing. She and Butler lived briefly in Florida and then returned to Ohio. She died at the age of sixty-six on November 3, 1926; her husband died less than three weeks later.

At the height of her career, Annie Oakley was quite probably the best-known woman on the planet. And she took the American West to the world.

Ella Knowles Haskell

Attorney
1860–1911

The first woman attorney in the United States was admitted to the Iowa bar in 1869. By 1890, there were still only about fifty women practicing law in the entire country. Women were thought too delicate to be stern and strong in court, and they were considered too emotional to deal with the facts of a legal case. Besides, most people believed that a woman's place was in the home keeping house and raising children.

Ella Knowles was the first woman admitted to the bar in the state of

Montana. She lobbied the legislature in 1889 to change the law that kept women from practicing law in that state, and though the legislators expressed some concern, they admitted her to the bar. One of the judges who examined her was surprised at how well she knew the law and said she was one of the best applicants he'd ever examined.

Ella Knowles was born in New England and educated at home until she was a teenager. She attended a seminary for young women and then a normal school where she trained to be a teacher. After teaching for several years, she attended Bates College in Lewiston, Maine, although higher education was generally thought wasted on women. They were just going to keep house, weren't they?

After graduation, Ella began to study law with a firm in Manchester, New Hampshire. In those days there were few law schools and the accepted way to study law was to work in a law firm. In 1888, poor health forced Ella to quit her studies and move West seeking recovery. She taught school in Helena, Montana, but once again decided to study law.

When she was admitted to the bar, Knowles had to build a practice. Young lawyers often began their practice by collecting debts, so she offered this service to several merchants. None accepted, but one, in exasperation, told her he had loaned two umbrellas to local women and if she wanted to collect them, she could. He never expected her to do it, but Knowles returned later that day carrying the umbrellas and demanding a fee of fifty cents. The embarrassed merchant protested, but other shoppers in the store supported Knowles's stand, and she was paid. Although the merchant had to apologize profusely to the two women who had borrowed the umbrellas, he began to use Knowles as his attorney.

Knowles almost lost her first court case, in which she represented a Chinese man who had been employed in a restaurant. The Chinese man claimed his former employer owed him five dollars. The restaurant owner produced a ledger that showed the amount had been paid. Ella thought she had lost, but then she had the idea of using a magnifying glass to examine the ledger. She saw that the figures had been changed, and the justice of the peace ruled in favor of her client.

By the early 1900s, she had built a large practice, with her clients being mostly men, and she was highly respected for her knowledge of the law. In 1892 she was nominated for state attorney general but lost by a narrow margin to Henri J. Haskell. Haskell was so impressed by her ability that he appointed her assistant attorney general in 1893. In 1895, the two were married, though they divorced within a few years.

Ella Haskell became president of the Montana Woman Suffrage Association in 1896 and often spoke out on women's issues.

In 1909, her health once again was poor, and she toured the world, hoping the rest would do her good. She died in Butte, Montana, on January 17, 1911, of an infection, leaving behind a large law practice and a good-sized fortune.

Evelyn Cameron

Photographer
1868–1928

By the late nineteenth century, photography was not usual on the frontier, but women photographers were rare. When she died in 1928, Evelyn Cameron, who went to Montana in 1889, left behind thirty-five leather-bound diaries and thousands of photographs. Her biographer, Donna Lucey, called the collection a "home movie of life on the frontier."

She was born Evelyn Flower on an estate south of London in 1868 and grew up with all the privileges of Victorian life in England—servants, governesses, and nannies, high tea, cricket, and foxhunts. But in 1889 she abandoned that life, to the dismay of her family, to marry Ewen Cameron, a Scot some fifteen years older than herself and in neither good health nor good financial shape. For their honeymoon, they went big-game hunting in Montana. At that time, a number of people from Great Britain had settled in eastern Montana.

The Camerons were attracted by the wide and open land with its oceans of grass and its invigorating air. Ewen thought it was a perfect place to raise polo ponies. With financial partners, he imported a pair of Arabian stallions and expected to make a fortune. The horses did not do well at their first ranch on the Powder River, so they moved to another ranch near a railroad town. At the Eve Ranch, as they named it, they lived in a three-room log cabin, a far cry from Evelyn's family estate.

Evelyn loved the hardship of ranch life, but it soon looked like she and her husband would have to return to England. Their failing polo pony business ate up most of their money, and the United States financial panic of 1893 took the rest. To make ends meet—and avoid returning to England in disgrace—Evelyn began selling vegetables from her garden and took in boarders, including her brother Alec. Another boarder, an Irishman named Adams, introduced her to photography.

In 1894, Cameron bought her first camera by mail order. Between churning and cooking and washing and sewing, she began to study photography. Because of her husband's poor health, she also did ranch chores usually done by men—roping and branding, dehorning cattle, milking cows, breaking wild horses, and cleaning stables and corrals.

Her ranch workday often lasted from dawn to dark, and then she began her photography study, often developing her negatives until dawn came around again. She photographed the people she knew—cowboys, sheepherders, homesteaders, and wolf hunters—along with the Montana landscape

Evelyn Cameron took this photograph of sheep shearers.

and its animals. She had no telephoto lens and often had to take dangerous chances to get close enough to her animal subjects. Once, carrying bulky equipment, she climbed a steep cliff and dangled from its peak to photograph an eagle's nest with two eggs. Then she went back after the eggs hatched to document the growth of the birds.

Animals were of great interest to Cameron. On her ranch she kept a zoo—hunting dogs, cats, lambs, antelopes, hawks, and wolf cubs. Once she took home two orphaned bear cubs, eventually sending them to a London zoo. She also raised a pair of wolf cubs until Ewen declared them too dangerous to keep. The wolves went to a zoo at New York's Coney Island.

The polo pony business went from bad to worse. When the Camerons shipped horses to England, the Brits did not like the wild American horses or their brands, which were considered unsightly. When six horses died on an 1897 voyage, their polo pony business was over. Photography paid the bills. Cameron charged 25 cents a picture or $3 for a dozen.

Ewen's health became worse. In 1900 the Camerons returned to England, but the inactivity there nearly drove Evelyn Cameron wild. Teatime could not equal ranching. A year later, the couple returned to Montana. Six years later they settled on a ranch within sight of the Yellowstone River. Ewen died on May 25, 1915, of cancer of the liver and brain, and from then on, Evelyn ran the ranch alone. A traveling Englishman wrote that she was the "most respected, most talked-of woman in the whole of the state." Never described as English, she was considered a Montanan, and in 1918 she confirmed that status by becoming a U. S. citizen. She died in 1928, when her heart failed after a routine appendectomy.

Evelyn Cameron's life—and her photography—might have rested in obscurity without Donna Lucey. In 1978, New York editor Lucey was looking for photographs to illustrate a book on pioneer women. She saw a few of Cameron's images at the Montana Historical Association and was told that an elderly Montana woman—a friend of Cameron's—had a large collection of negatives stored in her basement. Lucy convinced the woman to share the treasure, and since then Cameron's photographs have been shown throughout Montana. They probably deserve national display.

Willa Cather

Author
1873–1947

Willa Cather was born in Back Creek, a small community in in the mountain ridges of Virginia and she lived her adult life in Pittsburgh and New York City, but Willa Cather is most identified with the plains of Nebraska. When she was ten, her family moved to Nebraska on the Divide near the Kansas border, and Cather went suddenly from a land of trees and mountains to a flat, endless prairie. At first, Cather missed the mountains and trees of Virginia, but as she rode her pony across the miles of tall prairie grass, she came to understand and love this new land.

The Cathers' neighbors on the Divide were Swedes, Czechs, Germans, French, and Scottish-Irish. During the two years she lived there, Cather learned much about the hardships of her neighbors' existence. They built their homes of sod torn from the land; they endured drought, blizzard, prairie fires, and armies of insects that ate their crops. But their determination eventually turned the grassland into a land of wheat and corn.

Cather later wrote, "My deepest feelings are rooted in this country because one's strongest emotions and one's most vivid mental pictures are acquired before one is fifteen."

The Cather family next moved to the town of Red Cloud, Nebraska, going from the prairie to a world of schools and churches and social rules. Young Willa defied the generally accepted standards of behavior by cropping her hair and wearing overalls.

In 1890, she entered the University of Nebraska at Lincoln where she wrote stories and reviews for the local papers. After graduation, she taught and worked as a journalist in Pittsburgh, Pennsylvania. Finally she moved to New York City, where she was on the staff and then managing editor of *McClure's Magazine* from 1906 until 1912 when she was nearing forty years of age.

Like many of her fictional characters, Cather felt she had to leave the confining atmosphere of a small town on the plains for the sophistication of the East. But she always went west for several months each year to be refreshed and find inspiration for her work. Although in her early life she showed interest in several men—there was a doctor in Pittsburgh who wanted to marry her—Willa Cather never married. She developed a reputation for eccentricity, dressing in black, mannish clothes and shunning publicity. She hated telephone calls and photographers because she believed they interfered with her writing time. Before her death, she destroyed most of her papers and left a will forbidding publication of her letters.

Cather, who has been linked with Hemingway and Faulkner as among the greatest U.S. novelists, drew attention with the 1913 publication of her first novel, *O Pioneers!*. This book captured in fine detail the hard life of the immigrant settlers on the Divide and pictured the immigrant women as strong in their harsh and lonely life. After the publication of *O Pioneers!* Cather was able to leave journalism and work full-time as a novelist.

The title page to Willa Cather's O Pioneers!

Her next novels—*The Song of the Lark, My Antonia, One of Ours,* and *A Lost Lady*—are also based on her Nebraska experience. In *My Antonia,* considered her best novel by many, the story of Antonia Shimerda, a Czech immigrant, is told by her best friend, Jim Burden, who leaves the land to become a corporate lawyer while Antonia raises a family in Nebraska.

Of Cather's fairly large output, one other novel is considered among her most significant, and it reflects her interest in an entirely different part of the American West. In 1912 she visited the American Southwest for the first time; thereafter she returned often to such New Mexico landmarks as Taos, Santa Fe, and the pueblo at Acoma. *Death Comes for the Archbishop* is her fictional account of the life of French priest Jean Baptiste Latour (1814-1888), who worked among New Mexico's pueblo Indians and in whose honor a cathedral was built in Santa Fe. In her novel, Archbishop Lamy responds to the mesa and desert lands of New Mexico as strongly as did characters Antonia and Alexandra to the Nebraska plains.

Although Cather wrote of places other than the American West—eastern cities, the Old South, even early Quebec—her best work grew out of her passion for the plains, the desert, and the big sky of the American West. She once suggested that she could tell men who wrote Western stories a thing or two about the Old West but they would never listen to her because she wore skirts and didn't shave.

Willa Cather died in New York City on April 24, 1947, and was buried in Jaffrey Center, New Hampshire, rather than the family plot in Red Cloud. She had first visited that New England community in 1918 to find solitude for her work on *My Antonia* and she returned almost every year after that.

During her lifetime, Willa Cather received many honors. She was the first woman to be granted an honorary degree by Princeton University and she also received honorary degrees from the universities of Nebraska, Michigan, Columbia, Creighton, California, Yale, and Smith. She was a member of the American Academy of Arts and Letters and received a gold medal from the National Institute of Arts and Letters. Her book *One of Ours* won a Pulitzer Prize in 1923, and in 1933 *Shadows on the Rock* won the Prix Femina American in France. She was posthumously honored by the National Cowgirl Hall of Fame and Western Heritage Center. Her works have been translated into many languages, and at least one, *O Pioneers!,* has been adapted for television.

The Willa Cather Pioneer Memorial and Educational Foundation in Red Cloud is devoted to educating people about Cather—her life and her art. The foundation owns seven buildings and sites prominent in Cather's writing and has a large collection of her personal letters and artifacts.

Lucille Mulhall

The First Real Cowgirl
1885–1940

Lucille Mulhall was America's first cowgirl. She was the first woman to rope a steer in the show ring—she did it better than most men—and the first to show off her riding skill in rodeos and Wild West shows across the country.

Lucille was born in 1885 in St. Louis, Missouri. By the time she was four years old, her family had moved to the Oklahoma ranch belonging to her father, Colonel Zack Mulhall. When other little girls in town were playing with dolls or reading storybooks, Lucille and her sisters and brothers—Agnes, called Bossie, and Logan, who were older than Lucille, and Mildred and Charley, who were younger—rode horseback, looking for stray calves hiding in the creek beds, riding the fence line to be sure there were no breaks where cattle could escape, and counting the cattle. By the time she was ten, Lucille could rope and ride with the best of her father's cowboys. In 1896, at the age of eleven, she was sent to boarding school in St. Louis to learn to be a lady. She hated the school.

In the late 1890s, when Wild West shows became popular throughout America, Colonel Mulhall saw a business opportunity. In 1899, he presented his own show at the St. Louis World's Fair. He gathered together the best ropers, riders, and steer throwers in New Mexico, Texas, and the Indian Territory (now Oklahoma). Among them was an excellent roper named Will Rogers from Claremore in Indian Territory. He went on to become a world-famous entertainer and commentator on American life, but at that time he was just an extremely shy cowboy.

Rogers taught Lucille to build a loop of soft cotton rope that she could spin in front of her, and to throw a vertical loop—the kind of big loop that horses can ride through. To do this, Lucille had to use a stiff hard rope, made from the maguey plant, and lay the loop out flat behind her on the ground. As a rider approached, she would fling the loop over her head.

In 1901, Colonel Theodore Roosevelt held a reunion of his famous Rough Riders in Oklahoma City. The Rough Riders were mounted soldiers who fought under Roosevelt in the battle of San Juan Hill during the 1898 Spanish-American War. Colonel Mulhall put on a show for the Rough Riders and allowed Lucille to ride in a scene that reenacted a cowboy-and-Indian battle and showed off her roping skills.

Intrigued, Roosevelt visited the Mulhall ranch a few days later. Lucille rode an outlaw horse for him, and Roosevelt asked her if she'd ever roped a wolf. Roosevelt promised her that if she roped a wolf, he'd invite her to his

Inaugural Parade when he was elected vice president. Three hours later, Lucille rode into the yard dragging a dead wolf at the end of her rope. When Roosevelt was elected vice president—William McKinley was the new president—the Mulhalls went to Washington, D.C., where Lucille and her father led the parade.

The Colonel began scheduling his show to perform at every opportunity. Lucille was the star and audiences loved her. At sixteen, she was blonde, fairly tall but slender, and a little shy. Her father was still reluctant to allow her to take part in the steer-roping because of the danger, but Lucille's pleading wore him down, and at a show in El Paso he allowed her to enter the roping event. She drew a huge Mexican steer, and on her first throw the rope snapped. Her brother, Charley, handed her another rope. She threw again, and this time, her loop held. When the timekeeper called the score, she had the best time of the day.

Lucille continued to star in appearances scheduled by her father. Often her younger brother Charley was her sidekick, but Lucille was always the star of the show. Sometimes she amazed the audience with fancy tricks done in the saddle—leaning down from a galloping horse to pick up a handkerchief or standing in the saddle. But she really made her reputation as a roper. When she roped, she rode Jesse, the pony she had trained so that she could guide him with her knees, leaving her hands free for the rope. She set new roping records almost everywhere she went. Lucille loved competing—the thrill of trying to rope a steer faster than the next contestant—but she also loved the cheers of the audience.

For Wild West performers, the most important arena was Madison Square Garden in New York City. To ride at the annual Horse Show there—a high-society event—was to reach the top of the profession. Lucille and her family were invited to perform in 1905. Will Rogers was also at Madison Square Garden. One night, Rogers made the throw of a lifetime in an incident that many say sent him on his way to national fame. An 800-pound (363-kg) steer with 5-foot (1.5-m) horns was being cut out for Lucille to rope when it escaped from the cowboys who were working with it and, panicky, decided it would be safer with the audience. It jumped out of the arena and into the stands. Lucille threw a rope and missed. Will Rogers came to the rescue, climbing into the stands and roping the animal. Alone and on foot, Rogers was no match for 800 pounds of angry cow, but he held on until a dozen cowboys came to help.

Back home in Oklahoma, Lucille received a surprise invitation. The Miller 101 Ranch of northeastern Oklahoma had invited the National Editors Association to visit the ranch, and the Miller brothers—Zack, Joe, and George—wanted Lucille to star in the show which would include rodeo competitions and Wild West show events. She accepted the invitation gladly.

The performance for the editors' association was such a success that the Miller brothers took their show on the road as the Miller 101 Wild West Show and Lucille traveled with them for several years.

By the time Lucille Mulhall was twenty years old, her father and the Miller brothers had all bowed out of show business. She decided to take the show in a new direction. She would present "Lucille Mulhall and her Westerners" as a stage version of rodeo. Instead of performing in large arenas, she and Charley would do miniature versions of their tricks on small stages. Touring with this show, Lucille met rodeo musician Martin van Bergen. They were married in 1908.

At the end of the 1915 show, Lucille, now thirty years old, decided to retire. She was not old, but she was tired. Life on the road with the show had been hard. She and Martin divorced soon after her retirement.

But there was one more big adventure in Lucille's life. In the early 1920s she met Texas rancher Tom Burnett. Burnett was captivated by the Queen of the Range, and they married. Lucille had luxuries she'd never dreamed of—

fast sports cars, expensive jewelry, and fancy evening gowns—but she was uncomfortable and out of place in a world of noisy parties that started early and ended late. Within a year, she was back on the family ranch, divorced. She lived the rest of her life on the Oklahoma ranch, occasionally coming out of retirement to ride in local celebrations.

Lucille Mulhall was killed in an automobile accident in December 1940. Her coffin was carried to a grave on the Mulhall ranch by a horse-drawn wagon.

Miriam "Ma" Ferguson

Governor of Texas
1875–1961

Miriam "Ma" Ferguson was the second woman governor in United States history, inaugurated only fifteen days after Wyoming's Nellie Ross, who barely earned the title of first woman governor. Ma Ferguson served two terms as governor and ran for a third but was defeated.

Miriam Amanda Wallace was born in Bell County, Texas, and attended Salado College and Baylor Female College. In 1899, at the age of twenty-four, she married James

Edward Ferguson and served as first lady of Texas during her husband's governorship, until he was impeached in 1917 during his second term.

In 1924, Jim "Pa" Ferguson could not get his name on the ballot for governor because of the impeachment, so he persuaded his wife to run. Miriam Ferguson would probably have been content to devote her energies and attention to her husband and children, as she had always done. When she first ran, she was pictured as the typical Texas mother, in gingham apron and sunbonnet—but she did what Jim wanted.

In her campaign speeches, Ma Ferguson assured Texans she would listen only to the counsel of her husband, and they would get "two governors for the price of one." She promised to clear the Ferguson name, outlaw liquor legislation, and outlaw the Ku Klux Klan. She won easily and was inaugurated on January 20, 1925, in Austin, where the atmosphere was circuslike. A long parade of limousines, mule-drawn wagons, and old-fashioned buggies preceded the governor-elect to the capitol, while a band played "The Eyes of Texas." Ma had given up her gingham aprons and sunbonnets for black satin, an ivory feather boa, and a feather-trimmed black hat. The country housewife was replaced by a sophisticated woman ready to govern her state.

Many claim that Ma Ferguson was governor in name only. Jim had the real power, and sometimes forgot himself so much as to say "I" instead of "My wife." Once, when an aide disagreed with him, he is supposed to have thundered, "Which one of us is governor?" The aide replied, "Neither."

But Ma Ferguson did assert herself. She refused one of Jim's recommended appointees because the man drank liquor and ran with wild women. One of her major concerns was reform of the prison system, and in her first twenty months in office, she granted a total of nearly 4,000 pardons of one kind or another—executive clemency, conditional pardons, full pardons, and changing death sentences to life in prison. She pardoned prisoners who suffered from tuberculosis, and on one "Juneteenth" she pardoned hundreds of penniless black prisoners—Juneteenth in Texas is June 19, the day the news of Emancipation reached the state during the Civil War. It is celebrated to this day in Texas, primarily but not exclusively by black Texans.

Ma's administration was peppered with scandal. Her enemies—or Jim's—made accusations of purchased pardons, and there were hints of shady financial dealings. The Fergusons were not wealthy people and could not live on the $4,000 annual salary of the governor, so Jim sought employment elsewhere, and there were charges that he used his influence to grant highway construction contracts and received money in exchange. There was even talk of impeachment, though it came to nothing.

Ma did not run in 1928, but when the Texas Supreme Court rejected Jim's petition again in 1930, she placed her name in the ring. She was defeated by Ross Sterling in a runoff, but this proved to be a blessing in disguise. When the Great Depression crippled the Texan economy early in the 1930s, Sterling was blamed and Ma looked like a savior.

In 1932, Ma ran again, promising lower taxes and lower state spending and condemning the wasteful ways of the Sterling administration. She won a second term as governor, and it proved to be much less controversial than her first term. She continued to parole and pardon convicts, but most voters realized that the fewer prisoners they had to support, the less the strain on state finances in the difficult days of the Depression.

After that term, Ma Ferguson retired from politics, but in 1940, at the age of sixty-five, she ran for governor one more time. She could not, she said, resist a popular call. The call, however, was not popular enough to get her elected.

Jim Ferguson died in 1944, and Ma retired to private life in Austin. She died in 1961 and was buried in Austin, next to the husband she'd followed all her adult life.

In the 1990s, when career women are everywhere and stay-at-home wives and mothers are almost rare, it would be easy to criticize Ma as simply her husband's obedient servant, running for governor because he told her to. But for a woman whose interests had been limited to house and home, she showed extraordinary strength and independence once she was in office. And she didn't do a bad job running the state of Texas either.

Etta Place

Outlaw's Partner
1875?–1940s?

Often described as hauntingly beautiful, Etta Place is the most mysterious woman of the nineteenth-century American West. No one knows where she came from and no one knows what happened to her after her years with Butch Cassidy and the Sundance Kid, the notorious Wild Bunch outlaws. Described as looking like a Sunday-school teacher and shown in the movie *Butch Cassidy and the Sundance Kid* as a schoolteacher, she was also an accomplished horsewoman and sharpshooter. Whatever her background, Etta chased adventure—and found a tarnished kind of fame—as the longtime companion of Harry Longabaugh—the Sundance Kid. Some say that Etta was hard and cruel, the brains behind the robberies. Other sources believe she was simply a lady in love with adventure and with one very attractive outlaw.

While other members of the Wild Bunch had brief relationships with women of poor reputation, Sundance apparently remained with Etta. Butch Cassidy never showed any interest in one particular woman, except Mary Boyd of Lander, Wyoming, his former girlfriend who married another man. The three—Butch, Sundance, and Etta—were a close threesome.

The known facts about Etta are scanty. By 1896, Etta was with Butch and Sundance at their Hole-in-the-Wall hideout in southern Wyoming. In 1897, while the "boys" worked on a ranch in Alma, New Mexico, Etta lived in that town with a Mormon family and taught school. In June, the Wild Bunch—Butch, Sundance, and others—robbed a bank at Belle Fourche, South Dakota. In 1898 they robbed a train near Wilcox, Wyoming, and Sundance and Etta hid at Robbers Roost, a Utah stop on the famous "Outlaw Trail"—a string of "safe places" for outlaws stretching from Wyoming to New Mexico. In September 1900, they robbed a bank at Winnemucca, Nevada, and it's likely that Etta held the horses during this robbery. By early October they were in Fort Worth, Texas, where the group posed for a photograph at the John Swartz studio. That now-famous photo led to their recognition by detectives and forced Butch, Etta, and Sundance to flee the United States.

They went to South America by way of New York City, where rumor has it Etta and Sundance were secretly married. Although there is no proof of a wedding ceremony, their so-called wedding photo is now famous and shows the beauty that many found so remarkable about Etta Place. The threesome sailed for Buenos Aires, Argentina on December 20, 1901.

From 1902–1905 they ranched in Buenos Aires and supposedly gave up the outlaw life. Rumor has it that Sundance and Etta secretly visited the United States and the St. Louis World's Fair in 1904. In 1905, though, they were back to their old ways, robbing the bank at Rio Gallegos. Etta, wearing men's clothes, is supposed to have played an important part in this robbery.

The biggest mystery, of course, is the final end of all three. Not many people believe that Etta Place died in the 1907 hail of gunfire that supposedly killed Butch and Sundance in Bolivia. Many historians claim that outlaw Kid Curry, not Butch Cassidy, died in Bolivia. Cassidy, they say, returned to live a law-abiding life in the northwestern United States.

By the time of that shootout in Bolivia, Etta was apparently back in the United States. One story is that she came back to be treated in Denver for appendicitis; another, more likely story is that she opened a respectable boardinghouse in Fort Worth, Texas, operated it under the name of Eunice Gray, and died there in a house fire in the early 1940s.

In spite of the difficulty of pinpointing the facts of Etta Place's life, she is remembered as a beautiful and refined woman. Her story is an exciting and dramatic version of the stories of many women who followed Western outlaws.

Nancy Cooper Russell

Business Manager
1878–1940

Nancy Cooper was warned against marrying cowboy and would-be artist Charlie Russell. Not only was he several years older than she and given to drink, but people told her that he would never make a living as an artist. Historians now agree that Russell might not have made a living or reached the fame he did without his wife, Nancy. As it is, Charlie Russell is considered one of the two greatest artists of the Old West—the other is Frederic Remington. Both men produced paintings and sculpture; Russell also produced numerous watercolors, and collections of his famed illustrated letters, housed in museums, are now available in book form.

Nancy Cooper was born in Kentucky. Her mother, Texas Annie Mann, had married Al Cooper at an extremely young age, and Cooper left the marriage even before Nancy was born. Nancy's childhood was hard. She worked in the family's tobacco fields as a youngster and, at the age of five, contracted diphtheria. For the rest of her life, her health was never good. Her mother married again, but the stepfather did not want to raise a child, so Nancy lived with her grandparents. In 1888 when her grandparents died, she joined her mother and stepfather, and in 1890 the stepfather, James Thomas Allen, moved the family to Helena, Montana, to seek gold. He left Nancy, her mother, and her stepsister in that city, promising to return for them as soon as he made his fortune.

Nancy did household chores for wealthier women for fifty cents a day, while her mother took in sewing. But when Nancy was sixteen, her mother died of tuberculosis. Her stepfather came to retrieve Nancy's younger stepsister, and Nancy was left on her own. Friends helped her get a position in the home of the Roberts family some 25 miles (40 km) from Great Falls, Montana. There she was treated so kindly that she called her employers "Ma" and "Pa." At their home, she met Charlie Russell.

Years later, Nancy recalled her first impression of him. He was "a man a little above average height and weight, wearing a Stetson hat on the back of his blond head, tight trousers, held up by a 'half-breed sash' . . . high-heeled riding boots on very small, arched feet. His face was Indian-like, square jaw and chin, large mouth, tightly closed firm lips . . . . Everyone noticed his hands, but it was not the rings that attracted, but the artistic, sensitive hands that had great strength and charm."

When he asked her to marry him, she answered no. But he refused to give up, and they were married on September 9, 1896, in the Roberts home.

Charles Russell painted dramatic scenes from the West.

At first, the newlyweds lived in a one-room shack on the Roberts property, but within a year they moved to Great Falls because Nancy thought it would be a better market for Charlie's paintings. He was no longer a cowboy but was trying to make his living as an artist; up to that point, he had not had much success, partly because he could always be distracted by the chance to have a friendly drink with other cowboys. Charlie was also generous and embarrassed to ask people to pay for his paintings, so he often gave them away.

Nancy, having known poverty as a child, was more ambitious and knew that Charlie's art could bring them a good living. She kept him out of the local saloons as much as she could, and she refused to let his friends into their home. She was soon disliked by many people in Great Falls, but that didn't bother Nancy.

A local storekeeper who sold Charlie's paintings told the couple that Charlie was not asking enough for his work and that Nancy should take over the bookkeeping. Nancy found that the higher she priced Charlie's paintings, the better they sold. She began to get hundreds of dollars for paintings that he had once sold for $25. Charlie was embarrassed by the prices she asked.

Nancy's next move up the ladder of success was to arrange for exhibitions in various cities across the country—Chicago, Denver, Charlie's hometown of St. Louis, and New York, where he exhibited at the important Folsom Gallery in 1911. By 1914, his work was in a major gallery in London. The days of worrying about money were behind the Russells.

The couple moved into a two-story home in Great Falls which today is the center of the C. M. Russell Museum. In 1916, they adopted a son named Jack. Nancy was too busy promoting Charlie's career to do much mothering, but Charlie adored the boy and spoiled him hopelessly.

Charlie was nearly sixty when he began to feel ill. The problem was diagnosed as a goiter on the thyroid gland, but he delayed surgery—no one was going to "slit his throat"—until it was too late. The goiter had damaged his heart, and he died of a heart attack in October 1926.

Nancy spent the rest of her life promoting Charlie's work. Although she was twice asked to marry again, she remained Mrs. Charles M. Russell. She died in Pasadena, California, on May 23, 1940.

History has not treated Nancy Cooper Russell sympathetically. Many people resented her relentless pushing of her husband, her determination to keep him from his friends, and her ambitious, businesslike ways. But Charlie Russell once said, "The lady I trotted in double harness with was the best booster an' pardner a man ever had . . . . If it hadn't been for Mamie [his pet name for her] I wouldn't have a roof over my head."

Jeannette Rankin

Congresswoman and Pacifist
1880–1973

Jeannette Rankin of Montana was the first woman ever elected to the United States Congress. As a member of the House of Representatives in 1917, she voted against the United States entry into World War I. But her most courageous act came over twenty years later when, the day after Japan's attack on Pearl Harbor, she cast the lone vote in Congress against declaring war on Japan.

As a youngster, Rankin spent her winters at school in Missoula, Montana, and her summers on the nearby ranch where she was born. She was the oldest of six—five girls, one of whom died in childhood, and one brother, Wellington, with whom she remained close all her life. Rankin was known for doing things most girls didn't do: when ranch hands were puzzled by a piece of machinery, she got it working again; when her carpenter-father couldn't rent a building in Missoula because it had no sidewalk, she single-handedly built the sidewalk.

She graduated from high school in 1898 and went to the University of Montana, where she earned a biology degree in 1902. But she was undecided about what to do next. She tried dressmaking and furniture design but neither suited her, and she turned down several marriage proposals.

Her brother, Wellington, was then studying at Harvard University in Boston, Massachusetts. She visited him and in that city saw the hard lives and working conditions of the poor people on the East Coast. When she saw children as young as six working in factories and families living in poverty and misery, she resolved to help the poor.

At the age of twenty-eight, after the death of her father, she moved to San Francisco where she worked among the poor. Next she enrolled in the New York School of Philanthropy, where she worked in the slums as part of her training. Back in the Northwest, she worked among the poor in Montana and the state of Washington.

In 1910, she made a discovery. The state of Washington was preparing for an election to determine if women had the right to vote. Rankin believed that if women could vote, the government would be more sensitive to the needs of the people. She began to work for women's suffrage—the right of women to vote—in Seattle. When the amendment passed in Washington, Rankin decided to return to Montana.

Home for Christmas in Missoula, she asked for permission to speak before the Montana legislature about the rights of women. The all-male legislature had often joked about giving women the vote, but Rankin considered it a serious issue. She spoke on February 1, 1911, and the lawmakers took her seriously. Four years later, women in Montana had the right to vote.

When Rankin decided to run for the office of representative from Montana to the U. S. Congress, her brother Wellington served as her campaign manager. She ran as a Republican; seven men also ran on the Republican ticket. The state was huge and the population was scattered on ranches rather than clustered in cities as they were in the East. To reach her voters, Rankin had to travel thousands of miles. She spoke from train stations, street corners, at country fairs, potluck suppers, and one-room schoolhouses.

On Election Day evening, the Missoula daily newspaper reported that she was lagging far behind and had almost certainly lost the election. She went to bed bitterly disappointed. Over the next few days, however, more election results came in, and Rankin won by more than 7,500 votes. Newspapers all across the country reported that a woman had been elected to Congress for the first time.

Rankin took her place in Congress on April 2, 1917. Six days later, she was asked to vote on whether or not the country should enter World War I. In the first call for votes, she remained silent; in the second, she said, "I want to stand by my country, but I cannot vote for war. I vote no." Forty-nine other lawmakers also voted no, but Rankin received the most criticism, probably because she was a woman. Her people in Montana thought she was weak and unpatriotic, and the rumor went around that she had cried or fainted while voting. The country went to war.

During the next two years, Rankin worked for the causes she believed in: the needs of the poor and the right of women to vote. In 1919, the Suffrage Amendment passed, guaranteeing all women of legal age the right to vote. "If I am remembered for no other act," Rankin said, "I want to be remembered as the only woman who ever voted to give women the right to vote." She ran for re-election but was defeated—Montana had not forgotten her "no" vote over war.

In 1919, Rankin bought property in the state of Georgia and settled there to work for peace, organizing social clubs for children, forming the Georgia Peace Society, giving lectures about pacifism—the belief in peacefully working out differences between countries. During these years, she often visited Montana where Wellington, a prominent lawyer, had become one of the state's largest landowners and wealthiest ranchers. Her sister, Edna, is thought to have been Montana's first woman lawyer, and two other sisters were teachers.

As the 1940s approached, Europe was at war and many people thought the United States should join too. Rankin was by then nationally known as a pacifist. When she studied the international situation, she saw there was only one thing she could do—she must return to Montana and run again for Congress.

After a difficult campaign and much travel, she was elected to the House of Representatives in 1940. By now there were several other congresswomen serving their country, and they often followed her lead as she tried to introduce a peace bill, forbidding the United States to go to war. Each time it was introduced, the bill was voted down.

Then, on December 7, 1941, the Japanese attacked the U. S. fleet in the Pacific at Pearl Harbor. Countless ships were sunk and thousands of servicemen were killed. The country was enraged, and President Franklin Delano Roosevelt called for an immediate declaration of war. When she voted no, Rankin became the only lawmaker to have voted against both world wars. "As a woman I can't go to war," she said, "and I refuse to send anyone else." She was sixty years old.

After the vote, an angry mob followed her into the congressional coatroom, even though visitors were not allowed there. She had to hide in a telephone booth and call the congressional police to rescue her. Over the next few days, she was attacked constantly in the newspapers and in angry letters.

Even Wellington warned, "Montana is 110 percent against you."

When her term was over, Rankin did not run for re-election. Over the next twenty years she traveled frequently to India, to study the peaceful teachings of Mahatma Gandhi, and she often visited Montana. She also went to South America, Africa, Asia, and Europe. Between traveling, she was at her home in Georgia.

Jeannette Rankin (in front, wearing glasses) leads a protest of the Vietnam War during the 1960s.

In the 1960s when the United States entered the Vietnam War, Rankin, who had been publicly quiet for over twenty years, was back in the news. In 1968, the Jeannette Rankin Peace March moved through Washington, D.C., with eighty-eight-year-old Rankin helping carry the banner in front of the marchers. The march called attention to the fact that many people in the United States were opposed to the country's part in the Vietnam War.

Rankin remained active into her nineties and even considered running for Congress again, but her failing health confined her to an apartment in California, near the home of one of her sisters. She died in her sleep on May 18, 1973, at the age of ninety-three.

In 1990, a statue of Rankin was placed in the U. S. Capitol. An exact copy of the statue is in the Montana capitol. The words "I cannot vote for war" are carved in the base of both statues.

Jessie Daniel Ames

Reformer
1883–1972

Jessie Daniel Ames's most significant reform contribution came from her leadership in the Association of Southern Women for the Prevention of Lynching. At a time when the racially prejudiced Ku Klux Klan was powerful in the South and black men were frequently lynched by mobs of white men, Ames fought hard for racial equality. She sought an end to the abuse of black women by white men, and the end of violence against black men.

Ames grew up in Georgetown,

Texas, one of two daughters and two sons born to a harsh and strong father and a mother noted for her role as a community leader. Her mother was active in missionary societies and women's clubs, and consulted by her neighbors because of her healing powers. Ames's devotion to civil rights was largely due to her mother's influence.

She was married early, and unhappily, to a physician—Roger Ames—and they had three children, the youngest crippled by polio early in life. Roger Ames died after nine years, and soon thereafter Ames's mother was also widowed. Mother and daughter became a team, raising Ames's children and operating a local telephone company.

In 1916, encouraged by her mother, Jessie organized a county branch of the Texas Equal Suffrage Association, working to win the vote for women. She was one of those who made Texas the first Southern state to ratify the Nineteenth Amendment, which gave women equal voting rights with men. Ames went on to work with the Texas League of Women Voters and the Texas branch of the American Association of University Women.

She realized that her civil rights work was done among white women, and the organizations she led did not include black women and did not address racial problems. In 1924, she became a director of the Texas Council of the Commission on Interracial Cooperation (CIC) and began to work to bring black and white women together. Her belief was that women working together had a better chance of ending the injustice of segregation.

In 1930, she founded the Association of Southern Women for the Prevention of Lynching. Black women had long fought lynching but knew they would not succeed until they had the support of white women. The usual reason given for lynchings at that time was that a black man had in one way or another disgraced a white woman. Ames argued that this was rarely the real cause behind lynchings, and that attitude, while terrorizing black citizens, was insulting to white women. The anti-lynching organization circulated pledges (they got over 43,000 signatures), investigated lynchings, and publicized their findings through pamphlets and speaking tours. When possible, they actively interfered with lynchings in their communities, but their biggest weapon was to encourage women, within their own homes, to persuade men to stop the terrible practice. There was far less violence against black men in the Texas counties where the organization was most active.

Ames had a difficult life and was unable to devote all her energy to her causes. She managed to send her son and daughter to medical school and to create a normal life for her crippled child; she nursed her mother through a last illness. Through all this, she took great pride in her public work. She was described as positive, determined, clever, and proud by those who knew her. But people also recognized that it was not easy for her to follow the leadership of others or to admit to mistakes.

When the Commission on Interracial Cooperation was replaced by the Southern Regional Council in the 1940s, Ames retired from public life and moved to North Carolina. She remained interested in politics and world affairs but she was no longer the leader she had been for so many years. Reform efforts often move beyond their early pioneers, and in this case the civil rights movement advanced past the leadership offered by Ames. Still, she is extraordinary for her successful work in bringing an end to lynching in the South. Jessie Daniel Ames died in 1972 at the age of eighty-eight.

Edna Kahly Gladney

Pioneer of Adoption Reform
1886–1961

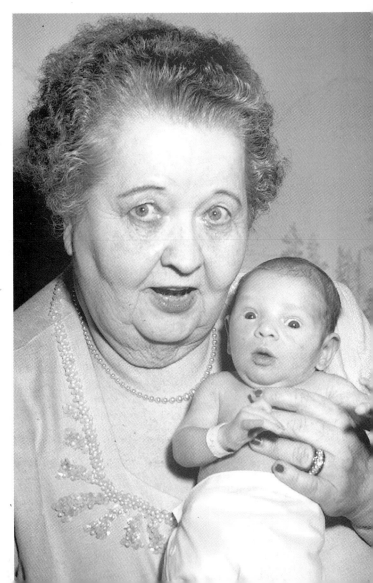

Edna Gladney, a woman with motherly instincts who was unable to have children of her own, forever changed adoption practices in the state of Texas and throughout the United States. Her life was made famous in a 1941 movie, *Blossoms in the Dust*, starring Greer Garson.

Even as a child in Milwaukee, Wisconsin, Edna Kahly worried about children who lived on the street. She often brought them into the family home for a bath and clean clothes. In 1903, she was sent to relatives in

Texas because her family thought the climate might be better for her lifelong respiratory illness. In Texas, she met and married Samuel Gladney, local manager of a flour mill.

The newlyweds spent several months in Cuba, where Sam had business, and his new wife surprised him by touring the leper colony. It was his first hint of the direction her life would take. The couple returned to Fort Worth, Texas, but in 1912 or 1913 moved to the city of Sherman, Texas, where Gladney began her civic work in earnest. She enlisted several women to help her expose conditions at the Country Poor Farm where the poor, the mentally retarded, and the physically handicapped were housed. The sheets were dirty, there were not enough beds, and orphaned children lived side by side with the sick and the mentally ill. After a newspaper article brought publicity but no change, the women, armed with brooms and mops, cleaned the facility themselves. Next they sent the orphaned children to the Texas Children's Home in Fort Worth, an institution that had placed over 1,000 orphans in homes.

Gladney next worked to open a day nursery in Sherman for the children of working parents, an increasingly common situation now that World War I was creating jobs for women. Six days a week, the nursery provided lunch, dinner, and supervision for the children. Sherman businesses gave funds, and Gladney put milk jugs on store counters all over town to collect donations for the nursery.

Samuel Gladney's finances were failing, mostly due to land and wheat bought on speculation. When prices dropped, Samuel went into debt. Much to the disappointment of Sherman residents, the Gladneys returned to Fort Worth and Samuel began to work to pay off his debts. Edna continued working on the board of the Texas Children's Home. When the director of the home died, Edna was named superintendent. She accepted the position, unpaid, for a year, hoping to get the home out of debt. She stayed until 1960.

Edna's first sought to change the language on birth certificates. If a baby's parents were unmarried, the certificate was permanently marked "Illegitimate." In 1933 Edna petitioned the state legislature to change the wording, telling them, "There are no illegitimate children, only illegitimate parents." Today, a baby placed for adoption is issued a birth certificate at birth showing the infant's natural parents' names. When the adoption is completed, the first certificate is sealed and a new one issued showing the names of the adoptive parents.

When Samuel died in 1935, Edna Gladney considered giving up her work with the children's home but was persuaded to remain. She began to take sociology courses at Texas Christian University and, although she never completed a degree, the university later gave her an honorary doctorate.

In 1941, Ralph Wheelwright, a publicist for Metro-Goldwyn-Mayer Studio in Hollywood, came to Fort Worth to adopt a baby. Wheelwright told Louis B. Mayer Gladney's story. Mayer became interested and made the movie, *Blossoms in the Dust*. Edna traveled to Hollywood, was treated royally, and became good friends with the movie's star, Greer Garson. Although the movie was not true to Edna's life—it showed her having a son who died young and an illegitimate sister who committed suicide, neither of which was true—Edna welcomed it for the publicity it brought the children's home. In an era of black-and-white movies, *Blossoms in the Dust* was one of the first dramatic films shot in full color.

With her share of profits from the film, Edna made plans to expand the home. Where the home had previously concentrated on the needs of infants and children, Edna convinced the board of directors to provide housing for birth mothers while they awaited the arrival of their children and a maternity hospital for their care in private. Edna strongly believed in privacy in adoption records and would have opposed today's open-records procedures. She was more than once threatened with contempt of court because she refused to release the records and names of either birth or adoptive parents.

The home's board of directors consisted of prominent Texas businessmen, but Gladney was not afraid to take them on when necessary. Once, when they hesitated to approve a recreation building, she said to them, "I just wish that all of you men were pregnant! I wish that you had to wear barrel-like clothes over your misshapen figures. I wish you had to live like this for nine long months—among strangers. Then I wish that you had your babies and had to give them up for adoption." They approved the building. In 1950, the board voted to rename the Texas Children's Home & Aid Society the Edna Gladney Home. Today it is the Gladney Center.

By the time Edna Gladney retired in 1960, the home was in sound financial condition and Gladney had received many honors. She was the star of a television episode of "This is Your Life" and was featured in articles in *The Christian Science Monitor* and *Women's Home Companion.* (The attention brought so many babies to the Gladney home that for a time the staff used dresser drawers as cribs.) Gladney was honored by B'nai Brith, Cal Farley's Boys Ranch, and the Carnation Company.

Edna Gladney died in October 1961 of complications of the diabetes that had bothered her for many years and caused her to weigh nearly 200 pounds (90 kg) and walk with a cane.

Her legacy lives on today in the Gladney Center in Fort Worth, a multi-million-dollar facility that has helped thousands of young women get their lives in order and has placed thousands of infants and children in loving adoptive homes.

Georgia O'Keeffe

Artist
1887–1986

Until 1929, Georgia O'Keeffe had spent only two brief periods of time in Texas and was a city dweller in the East. But on a summer trip to Taos in 1929, she gave her heart to New Mexico, and most people associate her bright, bold, dramatic paintings with that state.

O'Keeffe was born in 1887 in a Wisconsin farmhouse, the second of seven children. Both of her grandmothers were artistic, and the farmhouse held paintings of fruit that her Grandmother O'Keeffe had done.

When O'Keeffe had spent a few years at the same one-room schoolhouse her parents had attended, her mother decided that she wanted more training in art for her daughters.

Women at that time were not encouraged to be artists. They might teach art, and they might do decorative painting—such as china, small works for the home, and quilt designs—but they could never hope to have their work displayed in art galleries or museums. Mrs. O'Keeffe wanted her daughters to paint because she thought it would help them become refined society ladies, and she arranged for them to take lessons on Saturdays. The girls were taught by the traditional method: they copied paintings done by other people. But after the art lessons, O'Keeffe painted scenes from her imagination.

When she was in high school, the family moved to Virginia, and she was sent to boarding school. She continued to paint, sometimes drawing pictures of her teachers, and her watercolor painting of red and yellow corn won a prize.

After graduation, O'Keeffe's family sent her to Chicago's Art Institute to study. Sending a young woman to an art school where there were live nude models was a bold move, but O'Keeffe never developed a serious interest in painting people, nude or clothed. Nor did she ever paint living animals.

In 1907, she moved to New York City to study at the Art Students League. Her painting *Dead Rabbit with a Copper Pot* won a prize at the school. A realistic painting, it showed a dead rabbit stretched out next to the copper pot in which it would apparently be cooked. O'Keeffe was painting as others had, she had not yet developed her own style.

In New York, she met the famous photographer and gallery owner Alfred Stieglitz, but neither of them had any idea at the time how important their meeting would be. Later, he exhibited works of hers given to him by a friend—without O'Keeffe's knowledge.

In the next few years, O'Keeffe worked as a commercial illustrator in Chicago, suffered from and overcame an attack of measles that temporarily affected her eyesight, and studied art with several well-known teachers. One, Arthur Wesley Dow, taught her to think of composing a picture by dividing space into shapes such as circles and triangles. O'Keeffe began to experiment with her painting.

In 1914, she spent a summer teaching art in the public schools of Texas, and in 1916 she accepted an offer to teach at West Texas State Normal College in the town of Canyon. The school sat at the edge of the Texas Panhandle, high on the plains that border the Palo Duro Canyon. The landscape gave O'Keeffe a new experience—and a new artistic inspiration.

The plains were flat and endless, and the wind blew constantly. The sky was always bright and blue and clear under a blazing hot sun. There were crashing thunderstorms, with great bolts of lightning. And sometimes heat lightning tore at the sky at night, even when there was no storm. O'Keeffe's work changed dramatically to reflect this landscape. One of her earliest watercolors from this time is *Evening Star, III,* done in 1917, showing the first star to appear during a blazing sunset.

O'Keeffe and Stieglitz were now writing each other frequently, and he urged her to come to New York. He wanted to exhibit her work, and he wanted to be with her. She returned to New York in 1918 and they were married in 1924. For several years, O'Keeffe painted city scenes—a subject no one thought a woman artist would choose—and she painted bold shapes, such as the oversize, intense flowers for which she is now known.

O'Keeffe kept her own name after her marriage, and she and her husband were a dramatic couple—he wore swirling black capes, and she dressed severely in black with perhaps a white shirt. She pulled her hair into a bun at the back of her neck. Stieglitz took many interesting photographs of her.

In 1929, O'Keeffe accepted the offer of friends to spend a summer in Taos, New Mexico. The wideness and wonder of a land where the sky dominates fascinated her even more than west Texas had. She began painting the sights of the desert—mountains, sun-bleached bones, adobe churches, and desert flowers. Always she tried to capture the desert light. When she returned to New York, she brought back a barrel of bones to use as subjects for her painting. She was fascinated by their shape, texture, and color.

After that, O'Keeffe returned to New Mexico every summer, though she spent winters in New York with Stieglitz. He was twenty-three years older than O'Keeffe, and when he died in 1946, she moved to New Mexico.

Her most famous New Mexico paintings include a series on clouds, the 1930 *Ranchos Church—Taos,* and the *Cow's Skull: Red, White and Blue.* The cloud series was created after she was seventy-five years old. She hung the enormous canvases on the walls of her garage where she could study them. In all her work, the colors are bright and clear—she used a separate brush for each color to avoid any mixing or muddiness.

O'Keeffe lived to be ninety-eight. Over 900 of her works are owned by major museums, and she received many awards, including the United States Medal of Freedom.

Georgia O'Keeffe's work is important because she was a major woman artist when few women dared to be more than teachers of art. More than that, her work is important for its bold experimentation with color and shape. She used the images of the New Mexico desert and found beauty and unusual shape and line in ordinary things like bones and desert flowers.

María Montoya Martínez

Master Potter
c.1887–1980

She is known to the world today simply as María, the master potter. This woman from the small pueblo (Indian village) of San Ildefonso in New Mexico was invited to the White House by five different presidents, awarded a grant by the National Endowment for the Arts, received the American Ceramic Society's Highest Award for Lifelong Dedication to Clay, and given an honorary doctorate degree by Columbia College of Chicago. She also gave lectures and demonstrations at major universities. A retrospective show of her work with pieces representing her entire career was held at the Smithsonian Institution in Washington, D.C.

While these honors were appreciated, they didn't mean much to María. All she ever wanted to do was make pots and share with others what she knew about pottery.

María was born in San Ildefonso, New Mexico, and as a young girl survived a nearly fatal case of smallpox—"the spotted fever," as her people called it. In thanks, she and her father walked 10 miles (16 km) to make a pilgrimage to Santo Niño at Chimayo, where there was sacred dirt. To María, the dirt felt just like that from the *acequia*—or water ditch—at her home, the dirt from which she had tried to make pots.

Her early pots were made when she was only ten years old. She learned in the Indian way—by watching Tía Nicolosa Pena, her aunt. Soon María learned to add sand to the clay because it made the pots stronger and helped them hold together. And she learned to toss cornmeal into the four directions and pray to Mother Earth to guide her, so that she would do good work. When some of her early pots were nothing more than brown globs with holes in them, Tía Nicolosa told her that every potter has accidents.

Then María, who spoke only her native tongue of Tewa and Spanish, was sent to an English-speaking school, where she met a young man named Julián. But neither school nor Julián could make her forget about making pots. She made large pots, like her Old Grandmother had done before she died. And frequently, she found Julián watching her.

María and Julián married in 1904 and went to the St. Louis World's Fair to be part of an exhibition of Indian life, though María didn't want to leave her pueblo and certainly didn't want to sing and dance for people she didn't know. Before long, however, she and Julián were selling their pots, and María let the fairgoers watch her work.

After four months at the fair, they went back to the pueblo. Soon they had more money than anyone else in the pueblo, because they sold many pots. When others in the pueblo became jealous, María knew she must share the talent and the luck that Mother Earth had given her. Soon many women in the pueblo began to make and sell pots. María would sign her name to the best pots, but when a pot was sold she gave the money to the woman who made it. She marked her own pots by putting her handprint inside them.

One day Julián asked María if she was going to decorate a pot, and she said she didn't know how. It turned out that Julián knew how to paint pots. He began experimenting with designs, putting a matte or dull finish on a polished surface. Together they learned to make the ancient black pottery—blackened by smoking—that was once made in the pueblo. Legend has it that they made the first black pots by mistake when the fire went out and smoke colored the pots. After that, San Ildefonso blackware was their specialty, and Julián created designs to paint on the blackware with red slip—a mixture of red clay and water. His favorite design was the plumed serpent.

María and Julián had four sons—Adam, Popovi Da, called "Po," John, and Phillip. Their daughter, Yellow Pond Lily, died as an infant. Julián died in 1943, and for fourteen years Po was María's partner in pottery. She signed her pots "María Poveka" and those she made with Po, "María/Popovi." Po was also a talented painter and jewelry maker.

María continued to make pots and to teach others well into her nineties. She died at San Ildefonso in 1980. For María, making pots was very much a part of her culture and her life in New Mexico. Although she took her art throughout the United States—and it can be seen today in museums across the nation—she could not have made the beautiful pots she did without her New Mexican heritage and her strong feelings for Mother Earth.

Lillian Riggs

Ranch Woman
1888–1977

Lillian Riggs lived almost all her life on Faraway Ranch in Bonita Canyon in Arizona's Chiracahua Mountains. In later life, blind and widowed, she refused to leave the ranch or give up her daily responsibilities. In her eighties, she still rode horseback to check cattle. She also personally supervised the guest ranch at Faraway, which stands at the edge of a wild and fantastically eroded area known as Wonderland of Rocks.

Riggs's pioneer parents, Neil and Emma Erickson, settled in Bonita

Canyon just before Lillian's birth in 1888. Actually, Emma bought the property before they married with money she made running a boardinghouse. When they moved to Bonita Canyon, Neil Erickson built a stone house that was almost a fortress, with walls that were 3 feet (90 cm) thick and 10 feet (3 m) high and a door of double-thick boards of oak. The roof was made of cypress saplings covered with bear grass and topped with 2 inches (5 cm) of sand to make it fireproof. Bonita Canyon was once the territory of the Chiracahua Apache, led by the famous Cochise, and although most Indians were on reservations by then, there was always danger of an attack by a renegade—or runaway—band. Once the Apache Bigfoot came through Bonita Canyon and stole a horse from the Ericksons' neighbor. In 1900, the family moved into the box house, a two-story house with a winding staircase—very fancy for that time and place.

Although they lived simply and relied on Emma's vegetable garden for food, the Ericksons never had enough money and Erickson was often forced to leave the ranch to work as a carpenter. Emma then ran the ranch alone. She provided a model that her daughter, Lillian, would later follow. Hard work and solitude apparently did not bother either mother or daughter.

Lillian was educated at home until she was seven and then attended nearby El Dorado School. She went east to Galesburg, Illinois, for high school and then studied teaching at Knox College in Galesburg. She taught until 1917 when circumstances called her back to the canyon.

By then, Lillian's parents were living near Flagstaff, where her father worked for the Forest Service. Her sister, Hildegard, had turned their Bonita Canyon home into a guest ranch. Lillian did not like the idea of strangers living in her house, but she resigned her teaching position and returned to supervise the guest ranch. It was then that she named the ranch Faraway because it was so far away from everything—37 miles (59 km) from the nearest grocery store, for example. As Riggs reminded a granddaughter years later, "Remember, you are not in town where you can call a plumber, an electrician, a carpenter, a mechanic, or a blacksmith." Hildegard married and moved to California, and Lillian operated the guest ranch alone until 1923 when she married Edward Riggs, a widower with two children.

The story goes that Ed and Lillian, taking guests on a hunt, shot and wounded a deer. Not wanting to leave an injured animal, the couple went back the next day to find it. When the trail became impassable on horseback, they hiked—and thus accidentally discovered the fantastic rock formations now known as Wonderland of Rocks. The discovery of the rocks was a boon to the guest-ranch business. Ed established trails to these formations and displayed pictures of them in the nearby city of Douglas. Soon there was a move to make the Wonderland of Rocks a national park and, in 1924, President Calvin Coolidge declared the area part of the Chiracahua National Monument. One nearby mountain is called Cochise Head because its outline looks like the profile of a sleeping Cochise.

The guest-ranch business continued to grow, and the house grew along with it. During the 1930s, the lighting system was improved, a swimming pool was added, and various other improvements were made. In 1941, Lillian opened a Girl Reserve Camp at Faraway—a weeklong camp for children and young people's organizations. The camp provided dormitory space for 100 people, table tennis, guided hikes, dancing and campfires, all for $7.50 a day. Horseback trips to the Wonderland of Rocks were extra.

When Lillian's father retired in 1927, he and Emma moved back to the ranch. He died in 1937, but Emma lived to celebrate her ninety-fifth birthday and died in 1950. Ed Riggs also died that year, and Lillian was once again left alone to run the ranch. This time she had an added burden: she was blind, probably as a result of a bad horseback fall several years earlier.

Urged to sell the property, she said, "If I quit, how am I going to keep busy? . . . I don't want to give up this old home where I've met people from all over the world . . . . Nor do I want to give up my riding. When I'm in a saddle I feel I'm living again. I'm in no hurry to part company with my cattle either. Cows are so easy to keep happy." Asked how many head of cattle she ran, she replied, "The number of cattle I own is nobody's business. Do people ask their friends how much money they have in the bank or the amount they own in bonds or stock?" In the West, it's not polite to ask how many acres or how many cattle a rancher has.

In her eighties, Riggs never missed a roundup or a branding. At shipping time, though she could not see what was going on, she stood by the chutes while her cattle were weighed and loaded, listening to the details of the operation. When she rode to check her cattle, a companion rode with her and a guide rope connected the two. When she rode in a car, Riggs could always tell exactly where she was by counting cattle guards and turns in the road. With guests, she was a gracious and entertaining hostess, though some say that she was difficult and temperamental with her employees.

Assisted by her brother Ben and various friends, Riggs continued to operate the guest ranch until her health failed. She spent about a year and a half in a nursing home before her death in 1977. In 1979, the National Park Service purchased Faraway Ranch and closed it for restoration. The ranch was formally reopened in 1988 and now offers self-guided tours.

Angie Debo

Author, Historian
1890–1988

Sincerely
Angie

Angie Debo once said, "I've told more unpleasant truths about Oklahoma than anybody else who ever pecked out a name on a typewriter." Nevertheless, the state of Oklahoma has paid her high tribute. She is the only woman whose portrait hangs in the rotunda of the State Capitol Building, and during her lifetime she was affectionately known as the "First Lady of Oklahoma History," because she made a giant change in the recorded history of Oklahoma's Native Americans.

Angie Debo was born in 1890, just one year after the famous Oklahoma land run in which settlers rushed to take over lands that were previously part of the Indian Territory. With her family, Angie came to Oklahoma in 1899 and, as she later recalled, "watched wide-eyed as our covered wagon lumbered down the road under the warm sun and the big sky past the fields of greening wheat to the farm my father had purchased in the area opened to white settlement only ten years before."

She attended a one-room school and then spent "the most miserable years of my life" waiting for a high school to open. There were no libraries and usually the only book she had was the one her parents had bought for her and her brother the previous Christmas.

At sixteen, Angie passed a territorial examination and began teaching in a rural school—still without a high school education. When her hometown of Marshall opened a four-year high school, she returned as a student, graduating at the age of twenty-three. She went off to the University of Oklahoma in 1918, intending to major in English and become a writer. But history "happened to her." An unforgettable teacher, Edward Everett Dale, who was also the child of pioneers but was educated at Harvard, taught her how to write history. She went to graduate school at the University of Chicago, intending to teach, but found to her dismay that the history field was "shut, locked, and barred against women." Of the thirty colleges that applied to the University of Chicago for history teachers, twenty-nine said they would not take a woman under any circumstances. One said it would accept a women only if no men were available.

Debo became a writer without ever looking back at teaching, although she taught now and then at various institutions throughout her career. She returned to Dr. Dale and the University of Oklahoma for a doctoral degree. Her dissertation was published as *The Rise and Fall of the Choctaw Republic.*

Debo's most famous book is *And Still the Waters Run,* written when the

University of Oklahoma Press gave her a contract to write a history of Oklahoma Indians. The book that resulted was not at all what she—or the university press—expected. At that time—the 1930s—the only Indians most people saw were in silent movies, and no one even thought about Indian rights. Historians generally pictured Oklahoma before the land run as a vast open land, with only a few wandering Indian tribes.

Debo's research revealed that the Five Civilized Tribes—the Creek, Cherokee, Choctaw, Chickasaw, and Seminole—had their own system of land ownership and tribal government, both of which they believed were protected by treaty with the white man. Further, she discovered a criminal conspiracy to take control of Indian lands given in treaty to the tribes.

When white men learned that these Indian lands were rich in oil, they began to steal the land so fast that, in less than twenty years, white men owned 80 per cent of the Indian land. Some white men would seek out orphan Indian children and apply to be their guardians, robbing the children of their land for five or ten cents an acre (0.4 hectare). Others took advantage of adult Indians who could not read, write, or understand legal terminology. Among those Debo accused were the state's first governor, a United States senator, and the chairman of the Dawes Commission—the government commission that lied about Indian response to land "allotments." The Indians believed that carving up the land, as the commission ordered, would bring an end to their way of life.

As she wrote, Debo read chapters to her mother, who said, "No one will publish this, Angie." She was almost right: the University of Oklahoma Press refused the book as "too dangerous." However, in 1940, Princeton University Press published the book. Later, Debo would say that her goal was "to discover truth and publish it."

Except for occasional teaching experiences, Debo supported herself by writing, something that is difficult even now for all but the most famous authors. She did it all from the town of Marshall, Oklahoma, population 400, where she lived in the white frame house once owned by her parents. The badge of honor from her writing career was a large bump on the first knuckle of the second finger of her right hand—from years of writing research notes in longhand. Debo worked eight hours a day, six days a week. "I always took Sunday off," she said. "I felt I deserved that."

Laura Gilpin

Photographer
1891–1979

Laura Gilpin spent over sixty years photographing the American Southwest—its mountains, its deserts, and most of all its people—particularly the Pueblo and Navajo. When she gave her collection of photographs and negatives to the Amon Carter Museum in Fort Worth, Texas, over 20,000 negatives were cataloged.

Born in Austin Bluffs, Colorado, to a mother in poor health and a father who failed at one business after another, young Gilpin was educated in the East because her mother thought it important for her to have a cultured upbringing. All her life, Gilpin felt the inner conflict between her Eastern education, with its appreciation for tradition, and her Western independence and love of adventure. Returning home after studying photography in the East, she wrote, "I'm definitely a Westerner, and I just have to be in the mountain country. It's where I belong."

Gilpin was given her first camera—a Brownie box model—at the age of twelve. By her mid-teens, she had her own darkroom and was experimenting with color photography. Although she completed a twenty-eight-week course at the Clarence H. White School of Photography in New York, Gilpin followed her own instincts and interests throughout her career rather than basing her work on accepted photographic models or becoming part of any one school of photographers. She was interested in the land because of its effect on the people who lived in it, in contrast to most landscape photographers, who were generally men and who saw landscape in terms of its untouched beauty.

Gilpin's photographic career was uneven, often interrupted by the need to earn money for the support of her family. Twice she raised turkeys for income, and frequently she did commercial photography, even working briefly at the Boeing Aircraft factory during World War II. Sometimes she taught photography and she was the first and only instructor of photography at the Broadmoor Art Academy in Colorado Springs. Her work was shown in San Francisco, New York, England, and France.

In 1924, with friends Betsy Forster and Brenda Putnam, Gilpin made her first major visit to pueblos at Taos, San Ildefonso, and Laguna in New Mexico. She also visited Shiprock, Arizona, in Navajo territory.

On a 1931 trip to Arizona's Canon de Chelly, again with Betsy Forster, Gilpin ran out of gas and had to hike to the nearest trading post, leaving Forster to guard the car. When she returned, a group of Navajo were gathered

Bessie was licensed to fly on June 15, 1921, the first licensed black woman pilot in the world. Learning to fly wasn't enough for Bessie—she wanted to do stunts and aerobatic flying—but she was out of money. In September she settled again in Chicago; this time she opened a chili parlor.

Within a year, Bessie had earned enough money to return to France to learn aerobatic flying. She was the hit of European air society who admired her fearlessness and thought she was a natural stunt flyer. When she returned to New York in August 1922, *The New York Times* headline read: "Negro Aviatrix Arrives."

Bessie was a showman, specializing in such tricks as loop-the-loop, the Immelmann (a half-roll on top of a half-loop), figure eights, and the Richtofen glide (she cut the engine and let the plane glide, then pulled it up into barrel rolls). Air shows were popular in the United States, and Bessie always drew a large crowd, curious to see a black woman pilot. At a show at Chicago's Checkerboard Aerodrome (now Midway Airport), her engine lost power during a stunt and began diving to earth, coughing and sputtering. Even Bessie thought she would crash—but the engine caught. This even earned her the nickname, "Brave Bessie."

Another time, flying in a 150-mile (241-km) race from San Diego to Long Beach, California, the lights on her plane failed and she was lost. She landed in a field not far from Long Beach.

Many pilots in those days were barnstormers. They roamed the country, putting on shows in cow pastures. They would fly over a field to see if a crowd gathered. If that looked likely, the pilot would land, arrange to rent the field, and charge for rides—$4 for a ten-minute ride. Barnstormers attracted attention by outrageous stunts, such as flying through open barn doors or heading the plane right for a barn roof and pulling up at the last minute. It was dangerous but profitable work, and Bessie loved it.

Bessie Coleman's dream was to open a flying school for people of color.

She remembered her own anger, frustration, and humiliation when she was turned down, and she wanted to make sure other African-Americans could leave the cotton fields and soar as she did. At a show in her hometown of Waxahachie, she demanded that there be no separate entrance gates for colored and whites; but when she flew over the field, she was dismayed to see that the spectators had been seated in separate sections for blacks and whites.

Bessie Coleman's achievements were honored on a stamp in 1995.

Bessie's first serious accident came in 1925 when she tested a plane belonging to the Ford Motor Company. In that crash, she suffered broken ribs, a broken leg, and cuts and bruises. Her body took a long time to heal, but she was determined to fly again, and in 1926 she was back in the air.

In April 1926, she was to fly at a special show in Jacksonville, Florida, where there would also be a fair with a Ferris wheel, hot dog and lemonade stands, and balloons and music. She took off with her new mechanic, William Willis, piloting the plane. Almost immediately it was obvious that the plane was in trouble. When it flipped over at 2,000 feet (600 m), Bessie fell out of the plane to her death. To this day, no one understands why Bessie, usually so careful, was not belted into her seat. Willis stayed with the plane and was killed when it crashed. An investigation showed that a wrench had been jammed between the plane's gears.

Bessie Coleman paved the way for African-Americans who wanted to fly, and she was an inspiration to many. On the anniversary of her death, black pilots fly over her Chicago grave and drop flowers.

In 1995, the United States issued a thirty-two-cent postal stamp with Bessie Coleman's picture on it, giving her the place in history she so richly deserves.

Julia Morgan

Architect
1872–1957

Julia Morgan was an architect in an era when there were few women in that field. She was the first woman admitted to the famous Ecole des Beaux Arts in Paris to study architecture. In 1906, she designed the first house of reinforced concrete in Berkeley, California, and in her forty-seven-year career she designed more than 700 buildings. But her crowning achievement was the mansion—some call it a castle—built by William Randolph Hearst at San Simeon, California.

Morgan was born in San Francisco, the second child of a father who was a mining engineer. Her mother's wealthy family provided such luxuries as music and dancing lessons and frequent trips back East for Julia, her sister, and her three brothers.

Having an early interest in architecture, she attended the University of California at Berkeley, one of only a few women at that school and the only woman in the engineering program. The school had no architecture program at that time, but after her 1894 graduation Morgan worked briefly for a small architecture firm.

Many people claim that Hearst Castle in California was Julia Morgan's masterpiece.

In 1896, with the reluctant permission of her parents, Julia went to Paris to learn French and study for the entrance examinations to the Ecole des Beaux Arts. She finished 42nd out of 376 applicants and was admitted to the school. Morgan spent six years in Paris, barely finishing the program before the age of thirty. Students at the Ecole were not allowed to accumulate points toward graduation after they turned thirty.

When she returned to the United States, friends urged her to work in New York City, but she wanted to be in California. She loved its landscape, its rocks, trees, fruits, and flowers, and they would eventually influence her designs. She worked briefly with another architect and then opened her own studio. A modest sign on the door proclaimed, "Julia Morgan, Architect."

From the beginning, Morgan had wealthy and important clients and designed buildings for major institutions. She was the assistant supervising architect on the Greek Theatre as well as on a building for mining studies at the University of California at Berkeley that had been given by Phoebe Apperson Hearst in memory of her husband, Senator George Hearst. Morgan went on to design a bell tower and a library for Mills College—an all-women's institution—then a house at Berkeley for Kappa Alpha Theta, her old sorority. Over the years, she did many buildings for community-service programs and many buildings for women's programs—retirement centers, hospitals, YWCAs, and women's clubs. Commissions came from as far away as Hawaii and the Midwest.

It is difficult to characterize Morgan's style. She designed each building for its specific location and purposes, and her work includes English traditional and Mediterranean-influenced structures, as well as many buildings in the Arts and Crafts style, which stressed natural materials and simplicity. Morgan's buildings use a lot of stone and wood of various kinds, from gum to cedar.

But it was her work for the Hearsts that brought Morgan lasting fame. Her association with the family went back to the early days of her career. The Hearsts were newspaper owners and heirs to one of America's greatest fortunes. William Randolph Hearst decided in 1919 to build a home at San Simeon for his wife and five sons. Having worked extensively for Phoebe Hearst, William Randolph's mother, Morgan was chosen as the architect. She spent the next twenty years on the project. Almost every weekend she made the 400-mile (643-km) round-trip from San Francisco to San Simeon to climb up on scaffolding and down into ditches to make sure every detail met her standards.

The main house at San Simeon, with its two tall towers, seems to have been transported from Europe in the Middle Ages. Its bright white walls are ornamented with colored tiles, exterior sculpture, and carved balconies. Inside are huge murals, tapestries, carved fireplaces and furniture, and oriental rugs. Posts, banisters and stair railings are also carved with tiny details. The house has a theater, a billiard room, an indoor swimming pool, and a restaurant-sized kitchen. Morgan even had her own bedroom there.

Morgan also designed the other buildings on the property. When it was under construction, the most important workers had their own houses—designed by Morgan in Mediterranean style. There was a poultry-farmhouse for the servants who raised chickens, pheasants, and ducks for the Hearst table, a house for the gardener and tree man, and another for the head cowboy. Even before the main house was completed, Morgan supervised the building of guest houses—she called them "cottages," but we would consider them good-sized houses. The property also has hothouses, kennels, tennis courts, and indoor pools—all designed by Morgan, of course. The entire project was an enormous undertaking for any one architect, let alone a woman who stood barely 5 feet (152 cm) tall.

Morgan went on to do other houses for the Hearsts, such as the fanciful Wyntoon in Oregon with its striking exterior murals, and she also did other commercial buildings. But by 1950, most of her old clients had died, including Hearst, and there had been great changes in architectural style. There was no demand for her services, and because she had always worked alone, no one to carry on her work. In her later years, she became a recluse, living alone and seeing no one.

Mari Sandoz

Author
1896–1966

When Mari Sandoz's father learned she wanted to be an author, he wrote her, "You know that I consider writers and artists to be the maggots of Society." But Mari Sandoz turned the experiences of a difficult early life into lasting literature.

Sandoz was born in northwestern Nebraska on May 11, 1896, and spent most of her early life in the sandhills of western Nebraska—a treeless, stark, and frightening landscape. Christened "Mary," she was the oldest child of Swiss immigrants

Jules Sandoz and Mary Fehr. The family, who called her Marie, spoke German at home, and Sandoz spoke no English until she entered a one-room schoolhouse on the Nebraska prairie. Although she loved to read, Sandoz had only a few years of schooling and had to hide books she brought home. Jules Sandoz, a domineering man with a violent temper, disapproved of schools and books.

In spite of her scant education, Sandoz passed the eighth-grade examination and the teacher examination for the state of Nebraska in 1913, when she was only seventeen years old. She taught in rural schools until 1919, when she traveled far from the sandhills to enroll in business school in Lincoln, in eastern Nebraska. By 1921, she was taking courses at the University of Nebraska, and in 1923 she was a full-time student, determined to leave teaching and become a writer. As a writer, she dropped the "e" from Marie, changing the pronunciation entirely so that the accent was on the first syllable of her name.

Her student years were difficult for Sandoz. In spite of a small income from odd jobs, including work for the Nebraska State Historical Society, she was often hungry and depressed. She continued to write, and, like many writers, she collected a pile of rejection slips—later she would boast that they totaled 10,000. But she refused to give up, mailing her manuscripts to publisher after publisher.

In 1935, her first book, *Old Jules,* was published. It had been rejected by a dozen publishers when she submitted it for the Atlantic Monthly Prize. She won the prize,—$5,000—as well as national fame, and the book was published. After publication, the book also won a prize from the Book-of-the-Month Club. Although *Old Jules* is a biography of her domineering and abusive father, it also depicts the hardships of life on the Nebraska frontier for all settlers. Even as she feared him, Sandoz admired Old Jules for his part in building their community—and she recognized that it took men of his strength and determination to build frontier communities. The book is built largely on stories Old Jules had told his daughter. *Old Jules* shocked many readers, with its strong language, its unglamorous picture of frontier life, and its frankness about personal matters and family life.

Financially secure—or at least more so—because of the prizes won by *Old Jules,* Sandoz left Nebraska behind, moving first to Denver and then to Greenwich Village in New York City. She moved East, she said, to be near her publishers and near the major research libraries, but she disliked the East and went West to lecture and visit as often as she could.

Her writing never left Nebraska and the American West behind. She wanted to interpret life on the High Plains—the Dakotas, Nebraska, and Montana—for other Americans. Her themes throughout her writing were the land, how people affected it, and it affected people.

Sandoz wrote few novels—*Slogum House* (1937), the story of a power-hungry woman in the Nebraska sandhills, and *Capital City* (1939), a novel about unlikable politicians. But, in addition to *Old Jules,* she is remembered for three historical works about the Great Plains: *Crazy Horse* (1942), *Cheyenne Autumn* (1953) and *The Buffalo Hunters* (1954). *Crazy Horse* was one of the first books to treat the American Indian with sympathy and under-standing. (Crazy Horse was the Sioux Indian who led the charge against Major General George Armstrong Custer at the Battle of the Little Bighorn.) *Cheyenne Autumn* tells the story of the Cheyenne Indians' flight from the reser-vation. Both books reveal the author's closeness to the Indian community. She did not write about Indians as an outsider but as one who understood and admired them.

Sandoz wrote several other important books, including some for chil-dren—*Horsecatcher* (1956) and *Story Catcher* (1963), along with many articles and short stories that are a combination of biography, autobiography, histo-ry, and fiction. When she died of cancer in New York, her research files were given to the University of Nebraska library, where they are of great help to those who wish to study life in the American West. And Sandoz is said to have contributed to our literature the best and clearest picture of life on the High Plains. Her books are still read by young and old in North America, and they have been published in German, French, and Italian.

Mari Sandoz herself was a storycatcher—and a terrific storyteller.

Hallie Crawford Stillwell

Rancher
1897–

Hallie Stillwell has had many careers— teacher, rancher, mother, newspaper reporter, justice of the peace, author, store owner, museum curator, and Queen of the Terlingua Chili Cook-Off. Living on a remote ranch in the wild and majestic Big Bend Country of west Texas, she survived drought, rattlesnakes, mountain lions, screwworm epidemics in cattle, and Mexican raiders. She lost friends to influenza and herds of cattle to drought. Through all the hardships, she remained a natural lady, independent and imaginative and self-sufficient. Today she is known as the "Queen of the Big Bend," and her life demonstrates the wit and grit of Western women.

Born Hallie Crawford in Waco, Texas, in 1897, she moved with her family, led by a restless father, to several towns in Texas and even to New Mexico. But when she was twelve, the family returned to Texas permanently—with Hallie seated on a wagon seat and holding the lines of one of the teams of horses. After a journey of more than three weeks, the Crawford family unloaded in Alpine in far west Texas.

The family had a ranch in the Lajitas area, and Hallie attended high school in Alpine. After graduation and a summer at normal or teachers' school, she was qualified to teach. In 1916, she accepted a teaching position in Presidio, just across the Rio Grande from Mexico. The Mexican Revolution was at its height then, and Pancho Villa frequently raided Mexican towns. Hallie's father, concerned for her safety, declared that she was "off on a wild-goose chase." She replied, "Then I'll gather my geese." Years later, that phrase became the title of her autobiography.

Crawford taught school with a six-shooter tucked into the waistband of her skirt, hidden by her middy blouse. At night, the pistol was under her pillow. After a year in Presidio, she moved to Marathon where, on a blind date, she met Roy Stillwell. Because he was twenty years older than Hallie, her family did not welcome him or his flashy red-wheeled Hudson Super Six automobile. But the two were married on July 29, 1918.

If the Crawford family had doubts, so did the cowboys on Stillwell's ranch. They placed bets that Hallie wouldn't last six months on the remote ranch. She proved them wrong and won them over by her cooking, especially her biscuits. They even forgave her for scrubbing the coffeepot and ruining its well-seasoned flavor and for scrubbing the woodwork on which years of the ranch's records had been scribbled—which cow calved when and such important information.

The ranch was large and remote—the nearest town was Marathon, 40 miles (64 km) or two days by horseback away. But it was close to the Mexican border, and the men, who always feared Mexican raiders, would not leave Hallie at the ranch house alone. When they rode the range, she went with them. But Hallie's riding skirts and baggy trousers proved impractical. So Hallie, a woman of some size, borrowed the cowboys' pants, completing her outfit with a denim jacket, chaps, boots, spurs, a handkerchief around her neck, and a man's hat. But, she was quick to add, she always put on powder and lipstick.

The Stillwells had three children—sons Roy and Guy and daughter Dadie (Elizabeth Marie)—but even motherhood didn't keep Hallie from riding the range. Roy hired help to care for the children while Hallie did cowboy work. When the children were ready to attend school, Hallie moved with them to Marathon. There, not wanting to waste time, she got her barber's license and turned the front bedroom of the house into a beauty shop.

Roy Stillwell died in an automobile accident in 1948, and Hallie found herself in sole charge of the ranch and the family. When she heard that wax sold for sixty-five cents a pound, she hired Mexican workers to harvest candelilla plants, boil them in water and sulfuric acid, and skim off the loosened wax.

From 1956 until 1964, Hallie managed the Holland Hotel Restaurant in Alpine and also wrote stories and columns for several local newspapers. In 1964, she was appointed justice of the peace for Precinct I of Brewster County and over the years she performed almost 300 weddings, tried misdemeanor cases, and served as coroner. In 1979, she retired to open the Stillwell Store and Recreational Vehicle Park near Big Bend National Park. In 1991, she opened Hallie's Hall of Fame and Stillwell Ranch Museum next to the store. The adobe museum houses the Stillwell coat of arms with its motto, "Hold Fast," her Chili Queen crowns made of peppers, Indian arrowheads found on the ranch, certificates honoring Hallie, the .38 Colt she carried when she taught school, and other family mementos.

Honored by the Texas Press Association for fifty years of dedicated service to journalism, Stillwell is the author of two books—*How Come It's Called That?*, which explains place names in the Big Bend Country, and her autobiography, *I'll Gather My Geese,* which covers her life until Roy's death in 1948. She often said the sequel would be titled *My Goose Is Cooked.*

Stillwell was once quoted as saying, "There's something about ranch life that you don't give up. Everything I ever did was for the ranch. I can't imagine life without it. . . . I've been so hot I could have died. I've been so cold I thought I'd freeze. I've been so tired I thought I'd drop. But you just go on. . . . I don't know that I have accomplished great things, but I haven't been a failure."

Helen Gahagan Douglas

Actress, Singer, U. S. Congresswoman
1900–1980

Although she was born and raised in the East, Helen Gahagan Douglas became a Westerner when she followed her actor husband Melvyn Douglas to California in 1931. She served as Democratic congresswoman for California's Fourteenth District from 1944 to 1950, when she was defeated by future President Richard M. Nixon in what has become historically recognized as one of the dirtiest campaigns ever waged.

Born in New Jersey, Helen Gahagan was one of several children born to an Irish pioneer who made his fortune in the railroads and took his parental responsibilities seriously. Disapproving of his daughter's early ambition to be an actress, he sent her to private schools. Finally, she was allowed to be in a play one summer—with a chaperon at all times. Helen was expected "get her fill" of acting, but, instead, she was more determined than ever to go on the stage.

After overcoming—or at least softening—her father's objections, she went on to have a well-reviewed theatrical career. In her mid-twenties, she also wanted to sing and began a difficult training program. Over the next several years, she was hailed here and abroad as one of America's favorite actresses and singers and one of its most beautiful women. One reviewer wrote that she was "ten of the twelve most beautiful women" in the country.

On April 5, 1931, she married actor Melvyn Douglas, and they moved to California where he had a contract with movie producer Samuel Goldwyn. The couple had two children: Peter, born in October 1933 and Mary Helen, born in August 1938.

A lifelong Republican, Douglas followed the 1932 presidential campaign closely. The country was then in the midst of the Great Depression—resulting from the stock-market crash of 1929 in which Douglas, like thousands of others, had lost a small fortune. Even highly trained people were out of work, homeless and hungry, standing in long breadlines for food. At the same time, great dust storms swept across the Midwest, carrying away the topsoil and making farming impossible. Many farmers, fleeing what became known as the Dust Bowl, ended up in California, and Douglas was particularly moved by their plight. She toured the camps set up for migrant farmers and saw their hungry, hopeless children.

Douglas joined the Democratic Party, in which her husband had long been active, because of the New Deal—the social welfare programs proposed by President Franklin Delano Roosevelt. Those programs included the Works Progress Administration (WPA) which put people to work on needed public projects—such as building bridges and public buildings— allowing them to earn some income and self-respect. She served on the Steinbeck Committee (named after John Steinbeck, who had written the novel, *Grapes of Wrath*, about the plight of the migrants) to help provide aid. She was soon vice chair of the California Democratic Party.

By the late thirties, Hitler was marching across Europe. Douglas was among those who believed the United States should go to war against Hitler before he consolidated too many countries under his power and attacked the United States. When Pearl Harbor was bombed on December 7, 1941, Melvyn Douglas joined the U.S. Army. Helen Douglas continued to be politically active, and in 1944 ran for Congress.

She was a concerned and conscientious congresswoman, rising early each day and working late into the night. Douglas believed in racial equality—she fought the Daughters of the American Revolution over their refusal to let black singer Marian Anderson perform in Constitution Hall and she saw to it that the names of black soldiers who fought in the war went into the *Congressional Record*—in the face of loud objections by southern legislators. She was also concerned with atomic power and fought a bill giving control of such power to the military. She served with great interest on the Armed Services Committee.

Douglas was re-elected in 1946. That year, in California's neighboring Twelfth District, Richard Nixon unseated Jerry Voorhis, a longtime legislator, in a campaign designed to discredit Voorhis and make him appear to be a Communist. The Soviet Union was then gathering power and strength, and many Americans were terrified that Communism would leak into this country and Communists with Soviet sympathies would take over the government. Douglas fought in Congress against outlawing Communism, citing such action as a violation of the freedoms of speech, press, and assembly guaranteed by the U.S. Constitution.

In 1950, Douglas ran for the U. S. Senate; her opponent was Richard Nixon. In a campaign designed to smear Douglas as a Communist, Nixon cited her vote against outlawing Communism. Calling her the "actress-candidate," he accused her of voting 354 times with a New York congressman who was an avowed Communist. She had, but they voted on issues that were completely unrelated. Douglas ran her campaign on such issues as slum clearance, low-cost public power, rent control, and affordable housing—issues she thought the people wanted to hear about.

Dirty tricks were played on Douglas. At a rally, Nixon supporters doused her audience with water, effectively breaking up the crowd. Rocks were thrown at her house, and her husband's plays were picketed. One day, her daughter called her at the office in tears because of the awful things being said about Douglas on the radio. The final touch was flyers printed on pink paper that labeled her the "pink lady"—a Communist sympathizer. These flyers were waved at her everywhere she spoke.

Douglas maintained her dignity and refused to fight back on the same level. She knew, well in advance, that Nixon would rob her of her political career, but she was determined not to let him rob her of her self-respect. The day after the election, she later wrote, she awoke feeling free and whole, eager to go on with her life.

Defeat had come just before her fiftieth birthday. Although Douglas returned to the stage occasionally as an actress, her main activity for the next thirty years was speaking on behalf of issues and candidates she passionately believed in—including arms control, humanitarian issues, and Adlai Stevenson.

In later years, the Douglases lived in Vermont, where Helen Gahagan Douglas died of cancer at the age of eighty.

Tad Lucas

Rodeo Trick Rider

1902–1990

Tad Lucas rode into history in rodeo, a sport that is dominated by men. Lucas competed in rodeos for more than forty years, riding in every event she could, from steer riding and bronc riding to horse jumping and trick riding. She performed in England, Australia, Mexico, Belgium, and every state except Nevada. She worked with such rodeo "greats" as Gene Autry, Roy Rogers, and Tom Mix. Often called "Rodeo's First Lady," she was honored by the National Cowboy Hall of Fame, the

National Cowgirl Hall of Fame, and the Professional Rodeo Cowboy Association.

Born Barbara Inez Barnes in northeast Nebraska, Tad Lucas was the youngest of twenty-four children in her family. Some say she was called Tad, as in tadpole, because she was the last of that long line of children. Others say it was because she never crawled but, instead, scooted around on her backside. Whatever its origin, the name stuck to her for the rest of her life.

Growing up with so many brothers to encourage her, Tad rode calves and horses almost as soon as she could walk. Ranchers near Cody, Nebraska, used to bring their wild horses and calves into town on Saturdays to see if anyone could ride them. If it was a good ride, they generally passed the hat and took up a collection for the rider. Tad was thirteen when she first scrambled on a wild calf for the amusement of the people of Cody.

When she was fourteen, she rode a steer at the country fair rodeo in Gordon, Nebraska, and went home with the $25 prize for the cowgirls' steer-riding contest. Two years later, Tad saw her first rodeo cowgirl—Prairie Rose Henderson—and decided she too wanted to be a rodeo cowgirl.

In the early 1920s, Tad joined Frank Hafley's Wild West Show. With that show, she became the only woman ever to ride a Brahma steer in Madison Square Garden in New York City. Lucas won her first trick-riding trophy in 1925 at the Cheyenne (Wyoming) Frontier Days. That year she was also awarded the All Around Cowgirl trophy for her performance in bronc riding, racing, and trick riding. She went on to be Champion All Around Cowgirl and World's Champion Woman Trick Rider for eight straight years in Madison Square Garden and became the only permanent owner of the $10,000 Metro-Goldwyn-Mayer trophy.

In 1924, Tad married champion steer wrestler and bronc rider Buck Lucas. They settled in Fort Worth, Texas, and raised horses and two daughters—Dorothy and Mitzi. One of the earliest pictures of Mitzi—who weighed in at slightly over 2 pounds (0.9 kg)—shows her nestled in her mother's cowboy hat. Mitzi, literally raised in the rodeo ring, went on to become a well-known trick rider herself and to marry roper and quarter-horse trainer Lanham Riley. Buck Lucas died in 1960.

When Lucas began rodeoing, it was still the "bloomer era"—women wore bloomers instead of pants. She remembers they were often made of corduroy or satin and were fastened with elastic under the knee. Cowgirls wore brightly colored stockings, silk sashes around the waist, and matching scarves which they tied in a knot in front and let hang in a large triangle behind. The final touch on their outfits? A wide-brimmed Western hat, of course, probably a Stetson. Later, they wore leather-fringed skirts. In the 1930s, jodhpurs—pants that bloused at the hip and buttoned tight at the calf—became popular. Later, the women's outfits looked much like the men's—only with more flair, fashion, and sequins.

Small, charming, pretty, and "tough as a boot," Lucas stood only 5 feet 2 inches (157 cm), but she perfected many tricks that other riders wouldn't even try. Her most famous was the back drag. With her heels hooked into the saddle, she leaned backward over the horse's rump, her head only inches from its flying hooves. In another trick, she slithered beneath the belly of a running horse—under on one side and up on the other. More than once, she jumped a horse over a car. In 1933, trick riding was discontinued as a competitive event, partly because of the danger.

Fearless, Lucas rode in the Huntsville (Texas) Prison Rodeo and was the only outside girl permitted to take part in a rodeo billed as the "roughest rodeo in the books." She also tried rodeo clowning. A rodeo clown—it's always a man, except for Lucas!—works during the bull-riding event. His job is to distract the bull so that a thrown rider can safely leave the arena. Clowns often tease the bulls from a tire-covered red barrel, and Lucas was rolled around in that barrel so much that she was sore for a month after the rodeo.

Injured many times, Lucas suffered fractured feet, shoulders, and arms, as well as a broken nose and several cracked ribs. But her worst injury came in 1933 in Chicago when, attempting to go under the belly of her favorite horse, Candylamb, she lost her grip and fell beneath the animal's feet. The horse was moving too fast to stop quickly, and Lucas was tumbled along by the horse's feet. Her left arm was crushed so badly that it required six operations and was in a cast for three years. The rest of her life, Lucas had a stiff arm but she counted herself lucky to have use of the arm at all. In 1935, she rode in Madison Square Garden with her arm in a heavy cast with metal supports.

Between appearances, Lucas trained her own horses and owned a couple of dozen, all of which she kept until they died of old age. She rode Candylamb until that horse was twenty-five years old. When Tad Lucas retired in 1958, she said, "My horse was worn out, and I didn't feel like breaking in a new one."

One of her admirers today says, "If there was a Tad Lucas in the 1990s, women's rodeo would be in full swing."

And Into the Present . . . .

In the last half of the twentieth century, extraordinary women of the American West may seem less tied to the land than their earlier sisters. And their accomplishments often seem less influenced by their experience as Westerners. The days of challenge from a harsh landscape and harsher climates are long gone—modern technology makes it possible to live as comfortably in the Arizona desert or the Rocky Mountains as in New York City . . . unless you deliberately choose to face the land, as does Susan Butcher who races sled dogs. Increasingly, there is a sameness to our cities and the way we live. Dallas, they say, is nothing but New York City moved West.

Also, since the so-called feminist movement of the 1950s and 1960s made it more acceptable for women to leave their traditional roles and move into areas once dominated by men, there is a sameness to many women's accomplishments, no matter where they live. Women have proved themselves in politics and government, and women from Philadelphia and Boston are as likely to be astronauts or gymnasts or congresswomen as are Westerners. Ellen Ochoa, one of three female astronauts raised in the West, doesn't believe being a Westerner had any influence on her career, although she recognizes that California, her native state, is a place where many different ways of living are accepted—perhaps including a woman's presence in what is a strongly male profession. Still, she says, hers was a typical middle-class suburban childhood.

But there are still women whose achievements and accomplishments depend on their being in the West. Consider Wilma Mankiller, for example, former president of the Cherokee Nation, or barrel-racing champion Charmayne James-Rodman. Had they been born in New York City or lived in Florida, their lives would not be the same. Texas journalist Grace Halsell clearly traces the sense of adventure that has characterized her life back to a childhood on the open prairies of west Texas, and the work of artist Henriette Wyeth Hurd is tied to the New Mexico landscape of her home.

And in many western states there is still a strong tie to the state itself, an identification with its history and its unique characteristics. Don't try telling a woman in Fort Worth, where they treasure their cattle-drive history, that Texas is no different from any other state. And don't try telling a Montana ranch woman that her life is not affected by living on the vast windswept prairies. Many women of the West today still gather strength from their land and their heritage.

In some ways, however, all women today, from coast to coast, have inherited traditions of the extraordinary women of the West. Earlier Western women, from Sacajawea, Esther Morris, and Nellie Cashman to Bessie Coleman and Susan Butcher, have shown that women can do anything they set their minds to. These women blazed a trail that made possible the extraordinary accomplishments of women in the late twentieth century.

Babe Didrikson Zaharias

Olympic Athlete, Professional Golfer
1911–1956

Babe Didrikson Zaharias was a professional athlete at the time when all our sports heroes were men. A superb athlete, she also became a medical humanitarian by going public with her diagnosis of cancer at a time when few admitted to being a victim of that disease. But she was also "unfeminine," often loud and badly behaved, and a shameless braggart who had as many enemies as admirers. In many ways, Babe fit the stereotype of the larger-than-life Texan—except that she was a woman.

She was born Mildred Ella Didriksen (a misspelling in school records later changed it to Didrikson) in Port Arthur, Texas, the second-youngest of seven children born to Norwegian immigrants. They were a close family, and though Babe hated housework, she adored her mother. Her father, a sailor and cabinetmaker, held her spellbound with tales of adventure on the high seas, and it was probably from him that she inherited a tendency to make a good story better.

The nickname "Babe" came from the family, because she was the youngest child for several years. She would later claim, however, that she got the nickname in high school when she earned a reputation for hitting home runs in baseball. According to her story, people called her "a regular Babe Ruth" and the name stuck.

The family moved to Beaumont in 1914, and it was there that Babe grew up. She attended school in Beaumont and earned a reputation as a tomboy who loved to win at any game—baseball, marbles, racing, jumping, throwing, and roller-skating, which was her favorite. Known for getting into mischief and even for being a pest, she didn't hesitate to fight if offended and once accepted a challenge to a boxing match.

In high school she excelled at all sports and believed she could do anything, but she didn't fit in. She was not one of the boys, and she didn't belong with the girls either. As a result, Babe developed a lifelong compassion for outsiders. She also resolved to be the "greatest athlete that ever lived" and set her sights on the Olympics.

Because her family needed money, she left high school before graduation to work for Employers Casualty Insurance. The company had a semi-professional women's basketball team and believed sports were important to the well-being of its employees. Babe was a secretary, but her most important duties involved sports. She was only nineteen years old, earning good money, and sending a lot of it home to her family. She later completed her high school education.

At a 1930 American Athletic Union (AAU) meet, Babe set a record for the high jump and came in first in both javelin and shot put—and she did it all with a badly injured foot. In the 1932 meet, she won six events.

The 1932 Olympics brought Babe national attention. She was the star of the women's games, winning two gold medals, setting a world javelin record, and winning the 80-meter hurdles (she practiced by jumping hedges in Beaumont and had an unusual jumping style). Although her bragging offended her teammates, the newspapers loved Babe. They called her "Amazing Amazon," "Texas Tornado," "Betting Babe" and other names. In Texas she was honored as a conquering hero with parades, luncheons, and meetings with dignitaries.

Babe was careful to keep her status as an amateur, but the AAU ruled her a professional after she appeared in an ad for Dodge automobiles. She then began a pro career that included advertising, stunts, sideshows, product endorsements, a performance at Chicago's Palace Theater, and a women's basketball team called "Babe Didrikson's All-Americans." A 1933 film featured Babe in twelve sports—including football and boxing, though she would later say she only boxed and played football in staged photos. Babe was earning good money and still sending it home to her family.

At this time, Babe took up golf and announced that she intended to win the Women's Amateur Golf Championship in three years. She practiced until her hands bled, hitting balls for sixteen to eighteen hours a day. Although she always claimed she never picked up a golf club until after the 1932 Olympics, there is good evidence that she played golf in high school. Still, golf was a strange choice for a girl who, well into her twenties, had not yet outgrown her tomboyish ways and who often dressed like a man. Although golf welcomed women, it was a country-club sport, one noted for its refined manners and gentle ways. Once at a Texas State Women's Golf Championship at the exclusive River Oaks Country Club in Houston, a woman was overheard to say, "We don't need a truck driver's daughter here." Babe responded by clowning and acting even more masculine.

Because she had been a professional in other sports, Babe lost her amateur standing in golf and began to play in exhibitions and endorse golf equipment. She engaged a consultant to help with her image, bought new clothes at Neiman Marcus, and changed her hairdo, and even wore a girdle to a tournament—though she claimed it "choked me to death" and never tried that again.

In 1938, at the Los Angeles Open, she played with George Zaharias, a wrestler known as the Crying Greek from Cripple Creek. He was twenty-nine, weighed 235 pounds (106 kg), and was, according to Babe, "husky, black-haired, and handsome." Their courtship was soon public, although their careers drew them in different directions and the wedding kept being postponed.

Once she married, though, Babe became the American ideal of a good wife—buying furniture, taking care of George, and shedding her masculine image. And he became her protector—something she had never had. Within a few years, George suffered an injury that brought an end to his wrestling career, and he devoted his time to managing Babe's career.

As a female professional golfer, Babe found few tournaments available to her. She was frustrated. To keep busy, she took up tennis and then bowling, but she wanted to play golf. For the U. S. Women's Open in 1941, she played practice sessions with Bing Crosby and Bob Hope and proved herself every bit as good an entertainer as these two veterans. But World War II sidelined the golf world—public attention was elsewhere. And both of Babe's parents died in the early 1940s, events that were difficult for her.

Babe regained her amateur status by avoiding contracts for a certain length of time and she soon became the best-known woman golfer in the United States. Because she played golf like a man, with long, powerful drives, she forever changed women's golf. Folklore says her record is a 408-yard (368-m) drive, but it's known that 250-yard (225-m) tee shots were routine.

In 1945 she won the Texas Women's Open and the Western Open and went on a long winning streak. The British Women's Amateur took her to Scotland, where her behavior astounded the Brits. By 1947, she was the Associated Press's choice for Woman of the Year, and her career offers were so great that she took on a business manager. Reluctantly giving up her amateur status, Babe endorsed golf equipment that bore her name, a line of golf clothing, and even Timex watches. She also made a cameo appearance in a Katharine Hepburn movie. And what she didn't earn was given to her—hotel rooms, meals, almost anything she asked for—and Babe was never slow to ask.

The shortage of tours for women was still a problem, and Babe credited George with coming up with the solution. Pointing to the All-American Girls' Professional Baseball League, George suggested a similar organization for women golfers. The Ladies Professional Golf Association began with six members, Babe among them, and she served at least once as its president.

All was not well with George though. Inactive, he had gained an enormous amount of weight, and Babe talked about it to his face as well as behind his back. He could no longer follow her on the course but drove around the perimeter, honking the horn when she scored. Everything about him seemed to irritate Babe—his control over her career and money, and even his table manners, which had never been good but never bothered her before.

She turned for companionship to a young woman golfer, Betty Todd, who became her protégée, buddy, and partner. There were rumors about the nature of their relationship, but it appears that they were simply very close friends who shared many interests and who genuinely liked and respected each other.

Babe's career came to a crashing halt when she was diagnosed with cancer. Complaining of burning pain in her side, she was told she had a hernia; surgery fixed it. She continued to play, but her characteristic energy did not return. When the pain continued, the diagnosis of colon cancer was made. Within hours after a second and more serious surgery, she was entertaining the press at her bedside, telling her story, and warning well-wishers that she wanted no flowers. Donations, she said, should go to the Damon Runyon Cancer Fund.

Babe won seven tournaments after her surgery, but neither medical science nor her determination could lick "the black beast of cancer." She died on September 27, 1956, at the age of forty-five.

After her death, Babe was honored by the Texas Sports Hall of Fame; the University of the American Academy of Sports annually presents an award for courage in her name; and she was named golf's Player of the Decade. There is a Babe Zaharias Female Amateur Athlete Award, and the Associated Press's Woman Athlete of the Year Award is now called the Babe Zaharias Trophy. A 1975 movie, *Babe,* captured her life story, dwelling mostly on her marriage to George. In 1975, the city of Beaumont sponsored Babe Didrikson Zaharias Sports Week, and in 1976 the Babe Didrikson Zaharias Museum opened in that city. It houses her trophies and other memorabilia of the amazing career of an amazing woman.

Oveta Culp Hobby

Commander of the WACs, Newspaper Owner
1905–1995

Oveta Culp Hobby helped establish the Women's Army Corps (WAC), served as the first United States secretary of health, education and welfare, and ran a major big-city newspaper—the *Houston Post.* In addition to all that, she was one of the wealthiest and most interesting women in twentieth-century America.

Born in Killeen, Texas, Oveta was the daughter of lawyer and Texas legislator Ike Culp and pioneer suffragette Emma Elizabeth (Hoover) Culp. Oveta showed an early interest in the law, stopping at her father's office on her way home from school to read his legal texts. By the time she was ten, she had read the *Congressional Record* and, at thirteen, she had read the Bible three times. When Ike Culp was elected to the state legislature in 1919, he took his fourteen-year-old daughter with him to Austin, where she became a serious observer of each day's session.

In spite of classes missed while she was in Austin, Hobby graduated from Temple (Texas) High School and attended Mary Hardin Baylor College in Belton, Texas. In 1925, at the age of twenty, she was asked by the speaker of the Texas House of Representatives to act as legislative parliamentarian. She served in that capacity until 1931. During those years she was also active in politics, serving as an assistant to the Houston city attorney and even running for the legislature herself—but she was defeated.

Former Texas Governor William Pettus Hobby was a friend of Oveta's father, and she had known him all her life. They renewed their friendship in 1930 when she was in Houston, where the former governor ran the *Post-Dispatch*—a newspaper he would soon purchase and run as simply the *Post.* They were married on February 23, 1931, when she was twenty-six years old and he was fifty-three. Hobby liked to tell how Oveta's father warned him not to marry her, telling him, "She'll embarrass you. She doesn't give a hang about clothes." In later years, she was known as a fashionable dresser and a gracious hostess.

In the 1930s, Hobby was active in the newspaper, serving as assistant to the editor and publisher—her husband. She also survived two serious accidents. In the first, she was thrown from a horse and shattered her leg and wrist. She edited the newspaper's book pages from her bed and soon returned to the office on crutches. The second, more serious accident was the crash of a small plane carrying her, her husband, and several others. Hobby and other passengers saved her unconscious husband and the pilots by pulling them away from the burning wreckage, at great risk to themselves.

Meanwhile, Hobby was becoming involved in civic affairs—the board of the Houston Museum of Fine Arts, a member of the Junior League and the Houston Symphony Orchestra Committee, and regional chair of Mobilization for Human Needs. The Hobbys by now had two children—a son, William Jr., and a daughter, Jessica Oveta.

In 1941, General David Searles asked Hobby to organize a section on women's activities for the army, because with war on the horizon many women were asking what they could do to serve their country. Her initial refusal because of work and family obligations was overridden by her husband, who told her, "You must do whatever your country asks you to do." She studied the women's armies in France and Britain and prepared a plan for a women's army in the United States, along with a list of women who might command it. In the long run, she took the job herself, traveling constantly, speaking to large groups . . . and wearing the only WAC khaki uniform then in existence.

There were many prejudices against women in the armed services and limits on what they were allowed to do. Hobby, for example, was asked to join the Army-Navy Club, but only if she would enter by the back door! In spite of such difficulties, the WACs were vital to the war effort. By the time she resigned in 1944, Hobby's office had 600,000 requests for WACs, many more than the number of women available to serve.

Back in Houston, Hobby resumed her work with the *Post* and the family-owned radio and television stations. She also became active in organizations ranging from the American National Red Cross to the American Society of Newspaper Editors.

In 1952, when General Dwight D. Eisenhower ran for the Republican nomination for president, Hobby and her husband immediately became key figures in a national Democratic movement for Eisenhower. After he was elected, Eisenhower appointed her the first secretary of the Department of Health, Education and Welfare (HEW). As she had done with the WACs, she had to organize a new branch of the government. She was responsible for medical-research centers, hospitals for merchant seaman and drug addicts, an insane asylum and a leprosarium. She also distributed funds to colleges and ran teacher-student exchange programs with foreign countries. In addition, a variety of public concerns from cancer research to Braille books to worm control among Alaskan caribou, all fell under her administration. There was, she said, a "common thread of family service."

One of the major events of her administration was the announcement and distribution of the Salk vaccine for polio (infantile paralysis). This vaccine effectively controlled a disease that had killed or handicapped generations of Americans, including President Franklin D. Roosevelt.

In 1955, Hobby once again returned to the Houston *Post* as president and editor. Her husband was in poor health, and she spent the next few years taking care of him, bowing out of public duties except for her work with the newspaper. When he died in 1964, she resumed her activities in a variety of national organizations.

The list of awards given Hobby is too lengthy to list here. They ranged from the naming of the Killeen library in her honor to honorary degrees from the country's most important universities and appointment to the HEW Vietnam Health Education Task Force. She was also recognized for distinguished service to the advancement of human relations by the National Conference of Christians and Jews.

Hobby is remembered best today for three specific contributions—the WACs, HEW, and the Houston *Post*—and for her conviction that all Americans deserve equal opportunity, a conviction that guided all her work.

Henriette Wyeth Hurd

Artist
1907—

Daughter of the only real fine arts dynasty in the United States, Henriette Wyeth Hurd was raised and educated in the East, but like many before her, she followed her husband west—and became truly a woman of the American West. She is considered one of the great women painters of the twentieth century.

Hurd is the daughter of famed illustrator N. C. Wyeth, whose rich paintings of *Robinson Crusoe, Treasure Island,* and *The Boys' King Arthur* have charmed generations of children. Wyeth taught three of his five children and two sons-in-law to paint. Of the other two children, one is a composer and the other an inventor with countless patents to his name. The children shared a rich and stimulating childhood, and N. C. Wyeth once wrote, "I believe . . . that we, as a group, have got something, and that there is real promise of sound achievement—of major achievement—in the offing." Henriette recalls her childhood as extraordinary. "We were well disciplined, we had the best music, and our father talked about everything in the world—and with such enthusiasm!"

When she was three, Hurd contracted polio (infantile paralysis), which left her right hand so twisted that she can barely hold a piece of chalk in it. She draws with her left hand and paints with her right.

Of the three children who became artists, Andrew Wyeth (1917–), is recognized internationally as America's foremost realist painter. Daughter Carolyn (1909–1994), who lived at the family home in Chadds Ford, Pennsylvania, all her life, and painted primarily the surrounding area, is less well known than either her brother or sister, though she has been called the "strongest woman artist in America."

But it was Henriette who broke the family's Eastern tradition and married Peter Hurd (1904-1984), a student of her father's. Henriette had studied at the Normal Art School in Boston and the Pennsylvania Academy of Fine Arts, but her real teacher was her father, who was astounded at her ability when she was just a child. "Henriette drew a picture of a Japanese lily bulb we have here, and it was fabulously well done," he wrote.

In 1929, she moved with her husband to the Honda Valley of New Mexico, near the town of San Patricio. Since then, she has lived on the Sentinel Ranch there.

Henriette made the move against her father's wishes. He was afraid that marriage would interfere with her painting. She never allowed that to happen, although in many ways she embraces the traditional role of women. She believes that women "should read to their children, forget slim hips, and be happy. The more a woman gives to people and the busier she is, the happier she is."

Hurd has said that she always knew she was an artist. "We all drew, and I was quite certain I would be splendid. Even without my father, I think I would have gone ahead . . . ." Like her father, she believes in inherited talent. She once told an interviewer, "All our grandsons—everybody—is painting." Her two children—daughter Carol and son Michael—are painters, as are her grandsons, Peter de la Fuente and David Christian Rogers. Carol, Michael, and Peter also live in New Mexico and the family art—including works by Andrew Wyeth and his son, Jamie, who gained recognition early in life—is shown at the Wyeth Hurd Galleries in Santa Fe.

Hurd is best known for her still life paintings and for portraits that reveal the subject's inner truth—whether or not the subject wants the truth told. When she painted former first lady Pat Nixon, Richard Nixon so disliked the portrait's "wistful" quality that Pat Nixon asked the artist to change the expression. Hurd refused.

Hurd also painted many portraits of children. To keep them still, she would tell them stories of a fairy named Gardenia who had a rather bad temper. Once she asked a child with restless hands if she would hold them "just so"—in a way that Gardenia could sleep in them. The child sat motionless for forty-five minutes, until she said, "Mrs. Hurd, I think I ought to move my hands now." So Hurd said, "Gardenia! Wake up!"

Lady Bird Johnson

First Lady
1912—

Lady Bird Johnson has said she believes history will remember her only as the wife of President Lyndon Baines Johnson (LBJ). But many historians disagree, insisting that she will be remembered as an individual separate from her husband, and one who made many contributions to life in the United States. Her most important contribution is her beautification of America's landscape.

When LBJ suddenly became president after the assassination of President John F. Kennedy in 1963,

Lady Bird became the most active first lady since Eleanor Roosevelt. Her major project during LBJ's years as president was a national beautification program.

The project began with a Task Force on Natural Beauty, and the first target area was Washington, D.C., a city often described as "shabby." The city had major problems with pollution, highway location and construction, public transportation, and a decaying inner city.

Under Lady Bird's program, flowers were planted in traffic triangles and squares, awards were given for neighborhood beautification, and more than 9,000 azaleas were planted on Pennsylvania Avenue, In addition, the Japanese government sent roots for 4,000 cherry trees and a major donor gave money to improve a low-income housing area and to clean the city's many statues. In all, 25,000 new trees were planted in the city.

Lady Bird also focused on the nation's highways, and the 1965 Highway Beautification Act resulted from her work. The law requires states to control outdoor advertising along federally funded interstate and primary highways. At her insistence, the Bureau of Public Roads did a study which showed that there were over 16,000 junkyards along the nation's highways. The largest number of these in any one state—1,602—were found in Texas, Lady Bird's home state. These too were covered in the highway act. "Loss of beauty diminishes our lives," she told Americans, "and its presence enriches us."

Lady Bird was born Claudia Alta Taylor on December 22, 1912, in Karnack, a small town in east Texas. A nursemaid gave her the nickname Lady Bird when she was an infant, and she was never—in spite of some effort—able to shake it. Her father was T. J. Taylor, a businessman with interests in cotton gins, real estate, and a general store where he billed himself as "Dealer in Everything." Physically strong and personally dynamic, he was a strong model for his daughter, and she would later see resemblances between him and her husband. Her mother, Minnie Taylor, came from a privileged and cultured background in Alabama and found life in Karnack difficult. She was ill during much of Lady Bird's young life and died in 1918.

Lady Bird was raised by an aunt and spent much of her time alone, which may account for her lifelong battle with shyness. She graduated from high school at the age of fifteen—too young, she says—and attended boarding school in Dallas before transferring to the University of Texas at Austin. She received a B.A. in 1933 and enrolled for a second degree in journalism, determined to do anything to avoid returning to Karnack.

Lady Bird met LBJ in 1934. She was twenty-one, and he was twenty-six and secretary to U. S. Congressman Richard Kleburg. The two were total

Lady Bird Johnson was determined to make the United States more beautiful, even if meant planting wildflowers herself.

opposites—he was outgoing, ambitious, a "salesman," and Lady Bird was still shy. She was startled when he proposed on their first date, but she continued to see him. When he insisted they either marry or stop seeing each other, daring her to take a risk, she said yes and they were married immediately. It was November 1934.

The couple lived in Washington, D.C., and Austin, Texas, depending on LBJ's position, but settled in Washington when he ran for Congress in 1937. Life in the capital was very public for a private person. Lady Bird was expected to entertain LBJ's friends and colleagues at a moment's notice, yet she had no servants. Her husband was busy all the time, and she herself had official duties and all the social obligations of a congressman's wife. LBJ always encouraged her to be more outgoing and to spruce up her appearance, and she made determined and successful efforts at both.

During World War II, LBJ served as a naval reserve officer and Lady Bird took over his congressional office. She had a crash course in both business and politics and learned more in six months, she said, than she had in all her education. By 1942, all government officers were ordered back to Washington by President Franklin D. Roosevelt, and Lady Bird decided it was time to buy a house. When she thought LBJ's bargaining was going to ruin the deal for the house she wanted, she got angry at him—one of the few times on record.

With LBJ busy and no children to care for, Lady Bird needed a project. She bought radio station KTBC in Austin, using her inheritance from her mother, and spent six months straightening out the finances and personnel problems of the station. She owned it for twenty-two years, and every week in Washington she received a thick report on the station's activities. It's success proved her an able businessperson, and she won honors for leadership in broadcasting.

The Johnsons had two children—Lynda Bird was born in 1944 and Luci Baines in 1947—and in the 1940s and 1950s, Lady Bird was wife, mother, and businessperson. She remained active in Washington's political life and worked on the campaign when LBJ ran for the Senate in 1948—something that was unusual for politicians' wives at that time and particularly hard for the shy Lady Bird. She still dreaded making speeches, but a course in public speaking helped her to become a polished speaker.

In 1960, LBJ campaigned for the Democratic nomination for president but was beaten by JFK and then asked to join the ticket as candidate for vice president. Lady Bird became a major figure in that campaign because Jacqueline Kennedy was expecting a baby and could not campaign.

After the election, as second lady of the nation, Lady Bird set herself three goals—to help LBJ, to help Mrs. Kennedy, and to "become more alive" herself. The vice presidency brought many new experiences—foreign travel, ceremonial duties, and more formal entertaining.

In November 1963, President Kennedy was assassinated in Dallas, and Johnson suddenly became president. He served the remaining portion of Kennedy's term, then ran for—and won—re-election to a four-year term. LBJ was a controversial president, praised for his Great Society plan and its social programs to help the poor and underprivileged, and condemned for the Vietnam War. With the nation in turmoil over that war, LBJ decided not to run for another term as president. In January 1969, the Johnsons returned to Texas to live at their ranch on the Pedernales River. After a series of heart attacks, LBJ died on January 22, 1973.

For a brief time after his death, Lady Bird herself was in poor health. But she soon resumed an active public life, raising funds for the LBJ Museum and Library in Austin and serving on the University of Texas Board of Regents. She turned down an appointment to the United Nations and several other offers but she continued her beautification work. In 1982, she gave money and land to establish the National Wildflower Research Center near Austin. She was also instrumental in a highway-beautification program that has Texas highways wild with color in the spring when the wildflowers bloom. In Texas, she is the "wildflower lady."

LBJ could be charming and genial, and he could be loud and offensive, but there has never been any controversy about Lady Bird. As former Congresswoman Lindy Boggs once said, she is "too good to be true."

Dale Evans

Cowgirl Movie Star
1912—

oy Rogers and Dale Evans were the stars of countless Western movies in the 1940s and their names still seem inseparable, as though you can't say one without the other. And of course you'd have to add in Rogers's famous horse, Trigger. Yet Dale Evans had an independent and successful theatrical career before she met Rogers, and she continues to be known today for a variety of activities besides acting.

Born Frances Octavia Smith in Uvalde in southern Texas on October 31, 1912, she eloped at fourteen with her high school sweetheart. Not too much later, she found herself in Memphis, Tennessee—a single parent. Evans loved music, and she soon found jobs singing and playing the piano with local radio stations.

Always looking for a better job, Evans eventually went to Chicago where she sang with several orchestras and was featured in such famous hotels as the Camellia Room at Chicago's legendary Drake Hotel. Anson Weeks, an orchestra leader, hired her to sing with his touring musicians and took her to the West Coast where she sang at the famous Coconut Grove. Evans left the orchestra, though, to return to Chicago and sing for WBBM Radio.

When talent scouts discovered Evans, she was on her way to California and a Hollywood screen test for a movie with Fred Astaire and Bing Crosby. She didn't get the part—mainly because she wasn't a dancer—but she did get a one-year contract with Twentieth-Century Fox Studios. She played in two small pictures, and then signed on for a radio show that was broadcast nationwide; fellow performers included Don Ameche and ventriloquist Edgar Bergen (father of Candace Bergen) and his puppet Charlie McCarthy—all great stars of the 1940s.

Another screen test followed, and Evans played in several movies, including one John Wayne Western. So far, her career seemed to be a series of false starts—small movie parts, back to radio, then the movies again.

All that changed when the head of Republic Studios, Herbert Yates, decided to make a movie based on the stage play *Oklahoma!* Yates saw the lead male role as perfect for his biggest star—singing cowboy Roy Rogers. He knew Evans by reputation as a singer and assumed that if she was from Texas she could surely ride and rope, so he hired her for the female lead. Evans could certainly sing—but she could neither ride nor rope. In spite of that, *The Cowboy and the Señorita* (1944), was the first of twenty-six films Rogers and Evans made together.

Soon they were together as much off-screen as on. On New Year's Day 1947 they were married at the Flying L Ranch in Oklahoma, where they had just finished shooting *Home in Oklahoma.* Together they had an "instant family"—Evans's son, Tom; Roy's adopted daughter, Cheryl; and Linda and Roy "Dusty" Rogers, his children with his late wife, Arlene, who died in childbirth. Rogers and Evans had one child together—Robin—and a foster child, Marion, from Scotland. They also adopted three other children: Dodie, of Native American heritage; Debby, an orphan from the Korean War; and John David (Sandy).

Unfortunately, tragedy visited the family frequently. Robin died from complications of Down's syndrome; Debby was killed in a bus accident when she was twelve; and Sandy died serving with the military in Germany. Of Robin's life and death, Evans wrote the book *Angel Unaware.* She also wrote *Dearest Debby* and *Salute to Sandy.*

The 1950s were the heyday of Western series on television. Rogers and Evans formed their own production company and produced a half-hour show that ran for seven years. Both the television episodes and their major movies have been translated into many languages and are still shown today throughout the world. They also have appeared together at stadiums all over the world and in state and local fairs and rodeos.

Dale Evans has been named California Mother of the Year (1967) and Texas Woman of the Year (1970). In 1995 she was inducted into the National Cowgirl Hall of Fame and received the Cardinal Terrence Cook Humanities Award. She is equally proud of her three stars on the Hollywood Walk of Fame.

In 1996, Evans continues as an author, always working on a book, and has a weekly television show, *Date with Dale.* She takes an active part in the activities of The Roy Rogers-Dale Evans Museum in Victorville, California. And she is grandmother to sixteen children and great-grandmother to thirty. Roy Rogers died in summer 1998.

Grace Halsell

Journalist and Author
1923—

In 1952, when few women held jobs and most stayed home keeping house and caring for their families, Grace Halsell boarded a plane for Europe. She had a one-way ticket and $50 in her purse. She left behind her Texas home, her husband, and her job as a newspaper reporter. Halsell had no credit cards and no bank account. She planned to interview Texas soldiers and send the stories to their hometown newspapers. She wanted to prove that she could start from scratch, travel the world, and earn a living from the articles she sold. Her bold gamble was just the beginning of a life filled with more adventure than most people can imagine.

Halsell was born on the plains of west Texas, the youngest of six children. Her father, H. H. Halsell, was then in his sixties, and her mother was much younger. The father, a cowboy who had driven cattle up the trail and once fought off an attack by Apache Chief Geronimo, encouraged his youngest child "to travel, to get the benefit of knowing other peoples." She began her travels even before her European adventure by touring the British Isles by bicycle.

By 1953, she was back in Texas and working for Earl Baldridge, owner of Champlin Oil, as vice president in charge of communications. A picture from that era shows Halsell being hoisted to the top of an oil rig because she wanted to experience what she wrote about. After two years, she felt smothered by the oil business—and once again she walked away from a salary to prove that she could make her way around the world.

In Hong Kong, she lived on a fishing junk with a Chinese family of nineteen, most of whom had never lived on land. While in Hong Kong, she also wrote a column for the *Tiger Standard* newspaper. In Tokyo, she slept on tatami mats, ate fish, and took scalding baths in the Japanese style—all while she was a columnist for the *Japan Times.* Moving to South America, she traveled 2,000 miles (3,200 km) down the Amazon on a tug and crossed Peru's Andes Mountains in a jeep. In Lima, Peru, she became a columnist for *La Prensa,* the Spanish-language daily newspaper.

Working as a reporter in Washington, D.C., she was spotted by President Lyndon B. Johnson who immediately called her to the Oval Office. He wanted her to be a secretary for him, which he thought was a high calling for a woman. Halsell told him she could not take shorthand and he eventually made her a speechwriter.

But Halsell's greatest adventures began in 1968 when she left the White House. Wondering what life would be like if she had been born black, she took a medication to darken her skin and went to Mississippi. "I learned," she has said, "that the best job I could get, back then, was working for $5 a day as a maid." It was before integration, and she was once nearly arrested for using the "white" telephone in a bus station and later for attending a "white" church with a group of other black women. She wrote a book, *Soul Sister,* about her experience.

In the 1970s, having lived on a southwestern Indian reservation for a year, Halsell dressed in the clothes of a Navajo friend, Bessie Yellowhair, and traveled to California to work as a Navajo nanny for a white family. She wrote the book *Bessie Yellowhair* about this experience.

Some years later, with no passport or identification papers, she crossed with illegal immigrants from Mexico. Once she swam across the Rio Grande. Another time, led by a coyote—a man who makes a business of smuggling illegals into the United States—she darted across the dangerous Smugglers Canyon. She said it was her "most terrifying experience." Her book about these adventures is *The Illegals.*

In more recent years, Halsell has visited the war zones of Jerusalem and Bosnia, and she has stayed with *los viejos*—"the old ones," people in the mountains of Ecuador who live well over 100 years.

Why has she undertaken these dangerous adventures? Besides researching material for her thirteen books and countless articles, Halsell wanted to understand those less fortunate than herself by living as they did. "Becoming someone other than myself—while remaining myself—[is] within my life-long goal of living free from barriers of gender, color, creed, and race," she explains.

Maria Tallchief

Ballerina
1925–

A ballerina born on an Indian reservation in the American West? The two cultures—that of the Native Americans in the West and the sophisticated, European world of ballet—seem far apart. Yet those two worlds came together on June 29, 1953—Maria Tallchief Day in Oklahoma. The dancer, the guest of honor at a reception in her hometown of Fairfax, was treated to an Indian dinner of squaw bread, dried corn boiled with beef, and steamed beef. She was named Princess

Wa-Xthe-Thon-ba, Princess of Two Standards. And as she watched the Indian dances of her youth, Maria Tallchief felt the two cultures of her heritage and her life come together.

Tallchief was born in 1925 in the town of Fairfax, Oklahoma, on the Osage Reservation. Her father was Osage and her mother was Scottish-Irish. The family observed ceremonial occasions but did not live a traditional Osage life. They did, however, share with other Osage in the profits from oil being pumped from tribal lands. Tallchief's father invested his money in businesses, such as the Tallchief Motion Picture Theatre in Fairfax.

When Maria, called Betty Marie, and her sister were still fairly young, the family moved to California because the Mrs. Tallchief felt the small Oklahoma town did not offer enough training in dance and music. She was determined that Maria would play the piano, while Marjorie would be a dancer, but both girls studied piano and dance with professional instructors. And Betty Marie always knew that much as she liked piano, she wanted to dance.

At the age of fifteen, Tallchief studied with Madame Bronislava Nijinska, who selected her to be the principal soloist at a performance in the Hollywood Bowl. During that performance, Tallchief fell on stage! Nijinska told her stories of famous dancers who had fallen and said, "You must rise above it!" After graduation from high school in 1942, Tallchief got a bit part in a Judy Garland movie, then moved to New York City where she had an opportunity to dance with the Ballet Russe de Monte Carlo.

It wasn't always easy for her. A ballerina's life is difficult under any circumstances—long and rigorous hours of training, strict weight-watching, the disappointments of not getting this role or that. And for Tallchief, there were added difficulties: whispered comments about "a wooden Indian," suggestions that her oil-rich father would buy her a dance company so that she didn't have to compete. But Tallchief remained proud of her Osage heritage. Dancing with the Ballet Russe, she was urged to take a Russian name as so many others did. She refused and always danced as Maria Tallchief. And when she was a famous and renowned star, she was called "an Indian Princess" and "the beautiful dancing Osage."

At eighteen, she made her New York debut in *Concerto*. In 1946, she danced her first notable role—the Ice Queen in *Le Baiser de la Fée*, based on the Hans Christian Andersen story. That same year, at the age of twenty-one, she married George Balanchine, the choreographer who directed the Ballet Russe. When Balanchine left to form his own company, Tallchief danced with the Ballet Russe one more year and then joined Balanchine, who was a stern taskmaster but promoted her career. Their marriage was annulled in 1951, when she was twenty-five.

Tallchief's most outstanding roles were the Sugar Plum Fairy in *The Nutcracker Suite,* the Swan Queen in *Swan Lake,* and the legendary bird-woman in *Firebird.* In that role, audiences felt she was transformed into a flashing, soaring, flame-creature. Some critics suggested that the Firebird was the kind of being Tallchief's Indian ancestors might have worshiped long ago, which gave her greater power for the role. That role led to her position as prima ballerina of the New York City Ballet and her reputation, as *Newsweek* magazine described it, as "the finest American-born classic ballerina the twentieth century has produced."

Tallchief's sister, Marjorie, also had a distinguished career as a dancer, mainly in Europe, and the two women remained close.

In 1956, Tallchief married Chicago businessman Henry D. Paschen, Jr., and in 1966 she retired from the stage to be a wife and mother. In an art traditionally considered European, this American Indian from Oklahoma had shown that American ballet dancers could rank among the world's best.

Sandra Day O'Connor

U. S. Supreme Court Justice
1930–

In July 1981, President Ronald Reagan appointed Sandra Day O'Connor of Arizona to the United States Supreme Court. She took the oath of office on September 25, 1981, the first woman to be appointed to the highest court in the United States. Appointments are for life, so Justice O'Connor will sit on that illustrious bench until she retires.

Although O'Connor was born in El Paso, Texas, she grew up on the Lazy B Ranch in Arizona. The family lived in a four-room house with no electricity and no running water; the nearest town was 20 miles (32 km) away. When she was five years old, the child was sent to live with her grandmother in El Paso, so that she could attend school. She had already taught herself to read.

In El Paso, this girl who had grown up a tomboy missed horseback riding and the freedom of the ranch. When a brother and sister were born to her family, she insisted on returning to the ranch, but her high school was in El Paso. She graduated from high school when she was sixteen. O'Connor wanted so much to attend Stanford University in California, that she refused to apply anywhere else. She knew, however, that admission would be difficult. It was 1949, and the young men returning from serving in World War II took up most of the available places in college classes.

However, O'Connor was admitted to Stanford, where a course in business law convinced her she wanted to study law. She received the B.A. degree in 1950 *magna cum laude* (with great distinction). At that time, not many women were admitted to law school—she was one of only seven. O'Connor was given a prestigious appointment to the *Stanford Law Review* where, among other accomplishments, she coauthored an article with John Jay O'Connor III, a student who was a year behind her in school. In 1952, she graduated from law school.

Law firms at that time generally did not hire women and one firm even offered her a secretarial job. Finally, she was appointed a deputy in the office of the San Mateo County District Attorney, not far from Stanford. On December 20, 1952, she and John Jay O'Connor III were married at the Lazy B Ranch.

When her husband was drafted into the army in 1953, O'Connor became a lawyer for the U. S. Armed Forces so that they could be together in Germany for his three-year term of service. She took time out from the active practice of law to raise three sons—Scott, Brian, and Jay—but in

1965, when the youngest went to school, she went to work in the Arizona attorney general's office.

In 1969, O'Connor was appointed a state senator. In the senate, she helped strike down an old law that said women could work only eight hours a day while men could work as long as they pleased, and she changed a law that gave a man control of property belonging to his wife. O'Connor was known as an active fighter for women's rights. She ran again twice, and served as senate majority leader and on several major committees in the senate.

After three terms in the state senate, O'Connor felt her talents might better be used as a judge. She ran for and was elected as a judge for the Maricopa (Arizona) County Superior Court. People all over Arizona immediately recognized that O'Connor was always fair and that she followed the law to the letter. Governor Bruce Babbitt of Arizona then appointed her to the Arizona Court of Appeals, and she served in that court until President Ronald Reagan appointed her to the Supreme Court.

O'Connor is still known as a fair and dedicated justice. She has since been joined on the Supreme Court by another woman—Ruth Bader Ginsburg.

Ann Richards

Politician, Governor
1933–

Texas has long been a man's land. Its history is filled with the brave deeds of men such as Davy Crockett and Jim Bowie, who died at the Alamo, and General Sam Houston, who defeated the Mexican army to give Texas its independence. But as governor from 1991 to 1995, Ann Richards was a symbol for a new Texas, one that moved beyond the state's history of male supremacy. She became the second woman to govern Texas.

Ann Richards was born Dorothy Ann Willis on September 1, 1933, in the small community of Lakeview, central Texas. During the Depression, her parents raised chickens and grew their own vegetables. There was an occasional hog or duck in the yard, and fishing was done for food—not for sport. From her mother, Ann learned to make her own clothes, sometimes from feed sacks; from her father, Cecil Willis, she learned the art of storytelling, which would be important years later in her political career.

Cecil Willis was drafted into the U.S. Navy during World War II, and Richards and her mother moved to California—a great adventure for women in those days. For the first time she went to school with Latino and black students, and she found them to be just like anyone else. The experience may well have sown the seeds of the concern for civil rights that has been central to her career.

After the war, the family returned to Texas. Ann—skinny, scrawny and tall—played basketball in high school, excelled in debate, and went to Girls State, a program sponsored by the Women's Auxiliary of the American Legion in which high-school students conduct a mock government in the state capitol for one week. But the most important thing about high school was that Ann met a young man named David Richards.

The two were married by the time she graduated from Baylor University in Waco in 1954. When he enrolled in law school at the University of Texas, she taught social studies and history in a junior high school. The experience sparked a lifelong interest in education.

The young couple then moved to Dallas and started a family. Richards spent the next twenty years raising children. She also worked as a volunteer for the Democratic Party and helped found the North Dallas Democratic Women and the Dallas Committee for Peaceful Integration.

In 1969, the Richards family moved back to Austin. She was soon involved with the Zoning and Planning Commission and though she insisted she did not want an active life in politics, she ran Sarah Weddington's

1972 campaign for the Texas legislature. Weddington, a young Austin lawyer, had become almost instantly famous when she argued a successful and law-changing abortion case before the Supreme Court. Weddington's campaign had little money but lots of enthusiasm.

In 1975, Ann Richards then ran for county commissioner, using what she had learned in the Weddington campaign. She targeted voters who had a record of voting in small elections and sent them brightly colored post-cards (more likely to be read than letters), followed up by personal visits. She won the election easily, unseating a man who had held the job for twelve years. One of her first challenges was to make supporters out of the men on the road crews she would supervise. When she called a meeting to address them, forty big, frowning men attended—and one very ugly dog. Richards talked for thirty minutes, telling funny stories, asking about their families, trying without success to win them over. Finally she asked, "What's the dog's name?"

"Ann Richards," said a tough-looking man in the back.

She laughed . . . and they laughed . . . and the road crew were her friends. They renamed the dog Miz' Richards.

In 1977, President Jimmy Carter appointed Richards to the Advisory Committee on Women. Back in Texas, she spearheaded the organization of a traveling exhibit called "Women in Texas," convinced that, until then, Texas history had ignored its women. Later she helped organize a program known as Leadership Texas, designed to introduce young and promising female leaders to various aspects of life in the state.

Richards and her husband divorced in 1984, though they remain good friends. She also publicly acknowledged that she was a recovering alcoholic.

In the early 1980s, Richards ran for state treasurer. Once elected, she was invited to speak at national conferences and to campaign for Geraldine Ferraro for vice president in 1984 and for Michael Dukakis in his unsuccessful 1988 bid for the presidency. Introducing Ferraro, she was often asked to answer the question of whether Texas would vote for a woman. Her reply was, "My mama didn't call me Bubba!"

The highlight of Richard's growing national recognition came when she was invited to deliver the Keynote Address at the 1988 Democratic National Convention. The keynote is the first major address at a national convention. When she delivered the speech, Richards was already considering a run for governor in 1990. Eventually, she made the decision to run because she thought she could win and because she thought she could bring needed change to her state. Her opponent was a billionaire rancher and oilman named Clayton Williams, who put plenty of his own money into the race but who was not a politician and had no track record in government. Richards won by a slim margin—51 to 49 percent.

Richards immediately established a style for her governorship that included having fun. She became known for her trademark silver-white bouffant hairdo and her desire to ride a motorcycle. She often greeted visitors to her Austin office with the sincere question, "How are you?" delivered in a Texas accent. When she wanted to talk to legislators about an important school finance bill, she called them to the governor's mansion and served them cornbread and coffee while she talked.

Richards's accomplishments as governor were significant. She appointed more than twice as many women, three times as many Latinos, and five times as many black people as any previous governor. She fought and defeated a law allowing citizens to carry concealed handguns—a law that was passed by the next administration. She became known for making sudden midnight raids on dirty nursing homes to prove violations of health laws. She lobbied for—and achieved passage of—laws to limit rising insurance rates. She persuaded several major national companies to move to Texas, bringing over 7,100 jobs to the state. She shepherded the legalization of a state lottery to add much-needed money to the state's budget. She proposed tough ethics reforms to regulate legislators' activities. She forced a two-year stop on hazardous-waste sites. She added more than 60,000 prison beds and 12,000 drug- and alcohol-treatment centers.

In 1994, Ann Richards, surrounded by her family and standing on the porch of her childhood home, announced she would run for re-election. She ran against—and lost to—George W. Bush, son of the former president of the United States.

Although there had been much talk before that race of Richards as a possible vice presidential candidate, she dropped out of public life almost immediately after her defeat and began to work as a consultant in the private sector. Still, her colorful reign as governor and her outstanding accomplishments in that office speak eloquently of what women can achieve in the Western states of the United States.

Barbara Jordan

U. S. Representative, Legislator, Teacher
1936–1996

B arbara Jordan's life was one of "firsts." She was the first black woman elected to the Texas state legislature, the first to serve as governor-for-a-day in any state, and the first elected to the United States House of Representatives from the South.

Barbara was born in 1936 in Houston's Fourth Ward—a black community—and attended black schools, rode in the back of the bus, drank out of water fountains clearly marked for use by black people, and used black restrooms. As a child, she was unaware of prejudice and discrimination because she knew nothing else.

The Jordans were a religious and rather strict family—her father was a minister. Next to religion, music held the family together, and Barbara played the guitar. She was especially close to her maternal grandfather, a junk dealer and, as a child, she actively took part in his business.

As a teenager, Barbara was rebellious, wanting more than the strictness her home and church allowed her. In high school, she liked speech and debate and knew she wanted to stand out from her fellow students. A black woman lawyer, visiting her school, inspired Barbara to study law. At her 1952 graduation from Phyllis Wheatley High School, she was named Girl of the Year.

At Texas Southern University, an all-black school, she majored in government and lived at home to save money. Public speaking was still her strong point, and she traveled across the country with the debate team. These trips first brought home the realities of discrimination, when the team often traveled for miles and miles without finding a restaurant or restroom they were allowed to use.

Realizing she had to leave Texas and its segregated schools to get a better education, Jordan went to Boston University to study law. She was, for the first time, in an integrated world. She began to watch what worked: "White people . . . love to go have a cup of coffee." In Boston, she realized that education was not in knowing the answer but in the process of finding that answer.

With her law degree in hand, Jordan returned to Houston and practiced law for two years from the dining room of her parents' home, handling all kinds of cases—real estate, business, divorce, and adoption. When her small practice did not keep her busy, she worked for the local Democratic Party and encouraged black citizens to register to vote. By 1962, having made a name for herself in local politics, she had enough clients to open her own office. She shared a secretary with several other lawyers and filled her space with used furniture and framed color photographs of her political heroes—John F. Kennedy and Lyndon B. Johnson.

Barbara Jordan finally ran for political office herself because of her frustration at Houston's slowness to integrate its schools. Houston had desegregated its golf course in 1950, its library in 1953, city buses in 1954, but it was slow to act on school desegregation. She had learned from her own experience that separate schools for blacks did not provide equal education, and she wanted black students to have the best education possible.

In 1962, she ran for the Texas House of Representatives, although she had to borrow the $500 filing fee. She lost, although she drew out a heavier black vote than usual. In 1964, she ran again and lost again. Defeated but not discouraged, Barbara practiced law, remained active in the Houston Lawyers Association, and the Harris County (Houston) Democratic organization, and was soon appointed administrative assistant to a Harris County judge, the first black woman to be appointed to such a position. When she ran for the state senate in 1966, she finally won. By then, President Lyndon Johnson was one of her major supporters. He once said that Jordan "taught us that black is beautiful before we knew what that meant."

Barbara Jordan found herself in a state senate that was all male, all white, mostly Democratic, mostly conservative, and mostly lawyers. But she learned to use old prejudices to her advantage. Her first term was only two years and in 1968 she ran again, unopposed.

Barbara Jordan pursued her work in Texas, becoming a spokesperson for moderate blacks. "Wear an Afro if you will," she told young audiences, "but you were not born in Africa. You are not African. You are American." In 1972 she served as governor-for-a-day and was appointed the first black vice-chairman of the state Democratic Party. But now her sights were set on national politics.

Barbara Jordan was elected to the U. S. Congress in 1972. She quickly demonstrated her knowledge of such issues as oil allowances, cotton prices, and the Equal Rights Amendment. She even attended the delegation's weekly luncheon, which no woman had ever attended before. She worked twelve- to fourteen-hour days and was always present for a vote. Personally, she was known for not socializing and also for her sharp wit.

In 1976, she shared keynote honors at the Democratic convention with Senator and former astronaut John Glenn. In her speech, she talked of what it meant both to her and to the country that a black woman was given the honor of making that major address. During the Watergate scandal and the subsequent impeachment proceedings against President Richard Nixon, Jordan sat on the Judiciary Committee and reviewed the case carefully. Her passionate speech on behalf of impeachment was a major breakthrough—it was no longer possible for her colleagues to describe her simply as a black woman legislator. She had become an important national spokesperson.

Jordan served two terms in Congress, pushing for the Equal Rights Amendment and fighting for civil rights legislation. At the 1976 Democratic convention, she was one of several keynote speakers and her name was mentioned for vice president. But she knew it was time to leave politics.

In 1982, Barbara Jordan became a faculty member at the University of Texas Lyndon Baines Johnson School of Public Affairs. Although from that point on, the public saw less of her in newspapers and on television, she continued to be an active national voice. In 1994 she served on the U. S. Commission on Immigration Reform and received the Medal of Freedom, and in 1995 she delivered the Nancy Hanks Lecture on Arts and Public Policy. She was the seventy-seventh recipient of the Spingarn Medal for Enrichment of Afro-American Heritage from the National Association for the Advancement of Colored People.

Barbara Jordan never married, although she was always surrounded by many loyal friends. In her later years, a progressive neuromuscular disease, complicated by her size, confined her to a wheelchair. She died in 1996 at the age of fifty-nine of complications of her long-standing medical problems.

Although she sometimes had the reputation of being difficult—cold, aloof, and sarcastic—the truth was that she had no time for small talk and courtesies. Her eye was on the larger business. Her students valued her teaching, were extremely loyal to her, and relished the year-end barbecues at her ranch. In turn, her students were her greatest satisfaction; educating future public servants was more important to Barbara Jordan than all the firsts of her career.

Patricia Schroeder

United States Congresswoman
1940—

When Pat Schroeder, U.S. congresswoman from Denver, Colorado, decided not to run again in 1996, she was the longest-serving woman in the House of Representatives. She had served twelve terms—a total of twenty-four years—and had become known for her outspoken belief in such causes as family rights, civil rights, and women's issues. She was also known for her sharp but clever tongue.

A lawyer with a career in Denver and a mother with two young children to raise, Schroeder didn't intend to run for Congress in 1972. But her husband, also a lawyer, came home from a Democratic Party meeting and said, "Guess whose name came up as a candidate for Congress?" When she couldn't guess, he said, "Yours."

"What did you say?" she asked.

"How about *your* wife?" he answered.

But Jim Schroeder believed that his wife could win, even in a year when Republican Richard Nixon was expected to win by a landslide and anyone running as a Democrat in Denver was considered hopeless. Schroeder ran by talking about the issues she cared about—the Vietnam War, women's rights, family matters—and to her surprise, she won the election.

Pat Schroeder went to Congress with a six-year-old son and a two-year-old daughter. She was the only congresswoman with young children at a time when few women served in the House of Representatives or the Senate. It was still a time when people said women could either have a career or a family but they couldn't have both. Schroeder proved them wrong.

Born in Portland, Oregon, the daughter of a schoolteacher and an aviation-insurance man, Schroeder lived in Missouri, Texas, and Ohio before attending high school in Des Moines, Iowa. Her family encouraged independence, giving her, for instance, a monthly allowance as a fairly young child. If she ran out of money for school lunches toward the end of the month, she was told, "Too bad." She learned to budget.

Born into a flying family, she was an adventuresome and fearless tomboy who learned to fly by the time she was fifteen. Her father encouraged her to go to law school, but both her parents were somewhat nervous when she attended Harvard Law School. Even her forthright father confessed he was afraid nobody would marry her. The old saying, "You're nobody until you're Mrs. Somebody," still held true for women.

Schroeder married fellow law student Jim Schroeder in 1962, and they settled in Denver. In 1966, expecting her first child, Schroeder and her husband had a near-death experience because of a faulty exhaust on the furnace in their house. Although the health of the baby, Scott, was in question for several months after his birth, he suffered no long-lasting effects from the incident. Two years later, Schroeder gave birth to twins, both of whom died. It was an extremely painful experience and it gave her a feeling that no one was listening to what she was telling them about her own health. In 1970, she gave birth to a healthy daughter but again came close to death from complications afterward. These experiences contributed greatly to her determination to fight for women's rights to adequate health care.

Schroeder tried to stay home as a housewife and raise her children, but she freely admits that she failed in homemaking. To this day, she doesn't cook if she can avoid it, and she openly breaks the stereotype of the woman who keeps the house going for her husband and children. Her relationship to her children has been much more important to her than clean closets, home-cooked meals, and dusted windowsills, but she believes that raising children and having a career has kept her aware of the needs and problems of American families.

Her life changed dramatically in 1972 when she won her place in Congress. One of her first moves was to secure a seat on the all-male Armed Services Committee. When members challenged her because she had never served in the armed services, she had done enough research to say, "That gives us something in common." Most members of the committee had not served either. Schroeder noted that the committee talked a lot about protecting the women and children of America, but they never consulted women about their needs or wishes. Her early battles on that committee were for the rights of wives and families of servicemen.

In 1987, Schroeder was challenged to run for president. She announced her candidacy in June, spent the summer exploring the possibilities, and, in tears, announced she was withdrawing in September. She withdrew because she had neither the money nor the professional organization for an effective campaign. She was criticized for her tears—some said it set women's causes back, because it demonstrated that women cry and are therefore not capable of handling the responsibilities of a president. Schroeder replied that she would not want a president who was incapable of crying.

Schroeder is known as outspoken, sometimes even a troublemaker. Her most famous line occurred to her one morning during the Reagan presidency when she was scrambling eggs for her family. She noted that nothing—not a scrap of egg—stuck to the Teflon skillet, and it occurred to her that Reagan was a Teflon president: none of the scandals of his administration stuck to him. She used the phrase in a speech that day before Congress, and it has stuck to this day.

By leaving Congress, Schroeder was aware that she was diminishing the voice of women in that body, and she was unsure of her own future. She had twenty-four years in Congress, a Harvard Law School degree, and she was fifty-five years old. If she were a man, she said, she'd be in great demand by legal firms.

As it was, she left with an admirable record: she introduced and championed the Family and Medical Leave Act, fighting seven years for its passage. She backed such programs as Head Start, an early education program for poor children, and childhood immunization programs. She introduced legislation that would give parents a larger tax break for children and she fought for equal rights for women, people with disabilities, and victims of religious discrimination. Most of all, Pat Schroeder fought for the American family.

Wilma Mankiller

Chief of the Cherokee Nation of Oklahoma
1945–

Wilma Mankiller was the first woman elected chief of the Cherokee Nation in Oklahoma. The Cherokee are the second-largest tribe in the United States—only the Navajo are larger. The Cherokee have a population of 140,000 worldwide (they do not all live in Oklahoma), an annual budget of $75 million, and 1,200 employees. As chief, Mankiller is both a head of state, like President Clinton, and the chief executive officer of a corporation as complicated as General Motors or

American Telephone and Telegraph.

When she was first elected deputy chief in 1983, she thought she had gone as high as she could in tribal politics. But the chief—Ross Swimmer—left to head the Bureau of Indian Affairs in Washington, D.C. Wilma, a liberal Democrat, was appointed to take his place, and then won her own four-year term in 1987. When she ran again in 1991, she got 83 percent of the vote. Not that there weren't objections, however. Many Cherokee men felt threatened by the idea of a woman as chief. Her automobile tires were slashed and she received death threats. Now, she has won the respect not only of the Cherokee Nation but of the United States and the world, and she has done something for other Cherokee women. In the past, she said, "Young Cherokee girls would never have thought that they might grow up to be a chief."

Wilma Mankiller was born in Adair County, Oklahoma, on land known as Mankiller Flats that had been given to her grandfather in 1907. She is the child of a Dutch-Irish mother and a Cherokee father, farmers who raised ten children in a home without running water or electricity. Today, Adair County still has a higher percentage of American Indians than any other county in the United States.

Charley Mankiller—the name comes from warrior ancestors who were chosen to protect the village—told his children stories and legends of the old ways, of hunting with a bow and arrow and making canoes of tree trunks. And he told them of the Trail of Tears in 1838. The Cherokee were then one of the Five Civilized Tribes, so called because they had their own advanced societies. They were forcibly marched to the Indian Territory (now Oklahoma) from their homes in the southeastern United States, and many died along the way. But when the Cherokee arrived in Tahlequah, Oklahoma, they reestablished their civilization, with a complicated system of government, courts of law, and their own written language (unusual among

American Indians to this day). The tribe flourished until the Civil War, when they were treated as defeated Southerners and were forced to give up tribal lands to the Comanche, Kiowa, and others who were being herded onto reservation land. In 1907, their tribal lands disappeared completely when land was given to individual tribal members. It was then that John Mankiller was given the 160 acres (65 hectares) where his granddaughter Wilma lives today.

In the 1950s, the Mankiller family was relocated to San Francisco as part of a national attempt to move American Indians off the reservations and into mainstream society. Wilma Mankiller has said that coming from a poor, rural background, she suddenly had to deal with neon lights, television, and elevators. It was, she remembers, an extreme culture shock. But Charley Mankiller kept the tribal heritage strong for his family. He also became an activist, working for union organizations, doing community service, and talking politics. For his daughter, he was an inspiration.

Mankiller married a wealthy Ecuadorean businessman, and they had two daughters—Felicia and Gina. Mankiller then returned to school, studying sociology and community development at San Francisco State University. But she was, by her own admission, pretty much a stay-at-home wife and mother until one event changed her life.

In 1969, university students, in the name of the American Indian Movement, seized the old prison island of Alcatraz off the California coast to protest government treatment of American Indians. The Alcatraz seizure made Mankiller think about being an Indian. She began to study Cherokee history and tribal government, and she learned of the broken treaties and the despair. She became an activist.

In 1974, she divorced her husband and returned to Oklahoma with her daughters. There she worked to set up housing projects, programs for the elderly, and nursery schools—important rural services for the tribe. Her work was interrupted in 1979, when she was severely injured in an automobile accident. Plastic surgery repaired her smashed face, several surgeries mended her broken bones, and she barely avoided having one leg amputated. Her recovery took almost a year, a time she used for reflection. She still thinks of herself as the woman who lived before the accident and the one who lived afterward. Having come close to death, she wanted to complete the circle of life.

In 1980, barely recovered, Mankiller was diagnosed with myasthenia gravis, a neuromuscular disorder that causes extreme muscle weakness. Surgery and drug therapy were required to control the condition. Work became her best therapy, and she threw herself into tribal projects. Her dedicated work brought her to the attention of tribal leaders, especially Ross Swimmer, who asked her to run for deputy chief.

Mankiller faced one more physical crisis in 1990, when constant kidney problems indicated that she needed a transplant. One of her brothers was the donor, and the operation was successful. In spite of the challenges to her health, Mankiller felt she had so much to accomplish that she had to run for chief again in 1991. She consulted with her family, including her second husband Charlie Soap, a full Cherokee who is active in tribal affairs. The family supported her decision. Re-elected, she served until 1995 and continues to be active today in tribal and American Indian affairs.

Wilma Mankiller has achieved a rare balance—she has been able to move the Cherokee Nation ahead in the modern world without losing traditional customs, language, ceremonies, and culture. Under her direction, tribal services and income have increased dramatically, new construction projects have brought income and services, such as clinic buildings, to northeastern Oklahoma. There's a Job Corps Training Center, improved children's services, development programs for women on welfare, a reorganization of the Cherokee judicial system, a new tribal tax commission, and an agreement with the Environmental Protection Agency.

But Mankiller's achievements have gone beyond tribal affairs. A feminist who is accepted enthusiastically by men, she has become a national symbol as a woman as well as an American Indian. In 1987, *Ms.* magazine chose her as Woman of the Year, and her face has been on the cover of *Parade* magazine. She has received honorary degrees, given media and public presentations, and spoken on countless university campuses.

Even more important, Mankiller is a spiritual presence among the American people. Rather than focusing on what the Cherokee can learn from white Americans, she has shown non-Indians what they can learn from the Cherokee—a spiritual sense of the interconnectedness of things. And the renewal of her spirituality comes from the hardscrabble acres in northeastern Oklahoma known as Mankiller Flats.

Amy Tan

Novelist
1952–

Chinese-American novelist Amy Tan writes of the conflict between an Asian heritage and contemporary California culture, a conflict felt by many Chinese-American women. Her novels are particularly important to the many descendants of the thousands of Chinese immigrants who settled in California and, to a lesser extent, other parts of the West.

Born in Oakland, California, Tan is the daughter of a minister/electrical engineer and a vocational nurse. After graduating from San Jose State

College and doing postgraduate work at the University of California at Berkeley, Tan began a career as a technical writer. Working sometimes as much as ninety hours a week, she was unsatisfied with her life and decided to seek counseling. When the counselor fell asleep several times during counseling sessions, Tan became her own therapist and turned to jazz lessons and fiction writing as forms of relief. She began with short stories and then wrote her first novel, *The Joy Luck Club*, published in 1989. That book secured her reputation as an important young American writer.

The Joy Luck Club tells of June, a young Chinese woman whose mother and three friends belonged to a Joy Luck Club (Tan's own mother belongs to a similar Mahjongg club). When June's mother dies, the three other women persuade her to take her mother's place. Then they send her to China to inform family there of her mother's death. Reluctant to make the trip, June realizes that these women fear that she—and other young women her age—know little of the lives and heritage of the older women. It is a story, in many senses, about mothers and daughters learning to talk to each other.

Tan's next novel, *The Kitchen God's Wife*, has a similar theme. It is about a young California woman who comes to a greater understanding of her mother's Chinese background. The older woman, Mother Winnie, has made the barest adjustment to life in America. The daughter, Pearl, is more interested in the world of sports and fast food than in her mother's stories of life in China. Gradually, though, through stories of great hardship, Pearl sees her mother in a new light and discovers a new closeness to her.

Tan has admitted that these books brought her closer to an ethnicity from which she once tried to distance herself. She discovered "how very Chinese I was. And how much had stayed with me that I tried to deny."

Tan is also the author of a children's book, *The Moon Lady*, and has published stories in major magazines. Her next book, *The Year of No Flood*, will tell about a young boy's exposure to Western ideas in nineteenth-century China.

Susan Butcher

Sled-dog racer
1954–

Susan Butcher is the only woman—and one of only two people—to have won the world-famous Iditarod sled race four times. The Iditarod starts the first week in March from Anchorage, Alaska, and takes racers—they're called mushers—to Nome, over two mountain ranges, ice-covered rivers, the frozen Bering Sea, and dense forests. Along the way, mushers and their teams are threatened by violent snowstorms, temperatures that can go as low as $-50°$ F $(-45°$ C$)$ or as high as $40°$ F $(4°$ C$)$ (the great changes in temperature are as much a challenge as the extreme cold), and winds up to 140 miles (225 km) per hour.

Mushers must have at least seven and no more than fourteen dogs, and they are not allowed to change or add dogs during the race, although they may leave injured or sick animals at one of the designated checkpoints on the course. Mushers must carry snowshoes, a sleeping bag, an ax, booties for the dogs' feet, and food for themselves and the animals. Additional food is stored at checkpoints, and each musher is required to take one 24-hour layover at a checkpoint of his or her choice. Still, most mushers sleep only twenty hours in the twelve or more days it usually takes to complete the race.

Born in Cambridge, Massachusetts, Susan Butcher showed an early preference for animals over people and for country life over the city. Her father, a sailor and cabinetmaker, taught his daughters to sail and bought them carpentry tools when they were teenagers—training that Susan would later find most useful.

Susan was an athlete in high school—softball, basketball, field hockey and swimming—and was mildly dyslexic, which caused her difficulty with English but none with math and science. She had always had dogs, and at fifteen she bought her first husky or sled dog. When she bought a second husky a year later, her mother told her the family home was not big enough for the two dogs. Susan moved to Maine to live with her grandmother.

In 1972 she met a Colorado woman who bred and raced sled dogs. Deciding that sled-dog racing combined her two great loves—dogs and the outdoors—she moved to Colorado to help the woman with the care and training of the dogs. She also became a veterinary assistant, which gave her the knowledge she later needed to care for her own dogs in remote locations and in races.

Unfortunately one of her dogs was stolen in Colorado and the other was killed by a car. In addition, sled-dog trails in Colorado are found only in remote areas. In 1975, Susan moved to Fairbanks, Alaska, and was hired by the University of Alaska to work on a project to save endangered musk oxen. Already her sights were set on the Iditarod. She bought three dogs and moved with them to a cabin in the Wrangell Mountains, so remote that it was a "fly-in," accessible only by plane. For two years, Susan chopped firewood, hunted for meat, hauled her water from a creek, and mushed her dogs. The only time she saw people was in the summer when she went to Fairbanks to work on the musk-ox farm.

By luck the musk-ox project was moved to Unalakleet, Alaska, in 1977, and Butcher went with it. There she met Joe Redington, Sr., one of the organizers of the Iditarod and the owner of a large kennel. He helped Butcher get her first sponsor, and in 1978 she competed in her first Iditarod. She finished nineteenth, but won a share of the prize money that went to the first twenty finishers. In 1979, she finished ninth. She finished first in 1986, 1987, 1988, and 1990, came in second three times, and finished in the top five a total of nine times.

But there were bad years. In 1982, her sled crashed into a tree, badly injuring four of her dogs and bruising Butcher. Then a snowstorm wiped out the trail and drove her team 10 miles (16 km) off course. Several days later another snowstorm stranded her for fifty-two hours at a checkpoint. Nevertheless, she finished second to Rick Swenson—the other four-time winner and record-setter—and won $16,000 in prize money. In 1983, an ice surface broke beneath Butcher and her team and they were thrown into freezing water. She had to run along behind her team for several miles in order to stay warm.

Ironically, Butcher was not the first woman to win the Iditarod, although many people expected she would be. On the first night out in 1985, about 75 miles (120 km) northwest of Anchorage, she and her team were attacked by a moose driven crazy by starvation. The animal stomped and kicked the dogs for some twenty minutes, killing two dogs and injuring thirteen others. Butcher, who did not carry a rifle, fought the moose with an ax, but the attack was stopped only when another musher shot the animal. Butcher withdrew from the race to nurse her dogs back to health. That year, Libby Riddles became the first woman to win the race. But Butcher has said that her goal was never to be the best or the first woman. "It was to be the best sled-dog racer ever."

Butcher works hard with her dogs. She makes sure hers is the first voice they hear at birth, and she begins training early. Puppies as young as three months go on regular walks of 3 to 4 miles (5 to 7 km). At a year old, they are taken from the puppy pen and given their own doghouse; serious training begins then. She starts with short runs and builds the dogs up to 25 miles (40 km) a day, which means that Butcher herself travels many more miles, taking out five to ten teams a day. Before one of her dogs races in the Iditarod, it will have run 2,000 training miles (3,200 km).

But the dogs are also personal pets. Each dog is allowed into her cabin at the end of the day's training. She believes in training with love and respect, rather than fear. Butcher feeds the dogs a mixture of commercial dog food—she represents Purina—along with beef fat, liver, and vitamins. She carries their water from a creek.

In 1985, Butcher married David Monson, a lawyer and a musher and they live near Eureka, Alaska. It's still a remote area but now there's a gravel road to her house. "Where we're living is very downtown to me," she told an interviewer in 1987. Butcher and her husband operate Trail Breaker Kennels and own about 150 dogs, which they train and sell for anywhere from $150 to $5,000. Each summer, though, Butcher travels across the "lower forty-eight" states to appear at sporting-goods trade shows, meet with sponsors, and to speak at conventions and seminars. She has appeared on the *Tonight Show,* the *Today Show,* and *Good Morning, America.*

Butcher was named Female Athlete of the Year by the United States Sports Academy in 1987; Professional Athlete of the Year by the Women's Sports Foundation in 1987 and 1988; Athlete of the Year by the United States Academy of Achievement in 1988; Sled-Dog Racer of the Decade by the *Anchorage Times* in 1989; Outstanding Female Athlete of the World by the International Academy of Sports in France in 1989; and Top Professional Sportswoman of 1990 in the *USA Today*/United States Sports Academy Athlete of the Year competition.

In spite of her summer tours, Butcher has no liking for civilization as most of us know it. She doesn't have a television, doesn't use a clock or a calendar, and sees few people regularly. For months in winter, her husband is the only person she sees. He listens to the radio, she says, and reads *The New York Times*, which Butcher uses for kindling. "I'm not dependent on anyone for anything," she told a reporter. ". . . . If society as we know it disappeared, I know I could survive."

Ellen Ochoa

Astronaut
1958-

G rowing up in Los Angeles, California, Ellen Ochoa wanted at various times to be president or a lawyer or to do any job that would let her read a lot, because reading was her greatest pleasure. She was interested in space exploration, but in those days there were no women astronauts. She knew she would pursue a higher education, and she wanted to use that education, but, she says, it was a long time before she had a specific goal.

Ochoa graduated from high

school in La Mesa, California, in 1975 and received a bachelor of science degree in physics from San Diego State University in 1980. She went on to Stanford University, where she received a master of science degree in 1981 and a doctorate in electrical engineering in 1985. While in graduate school, she decided she wanted to be an astronaut, because there were now women in the program.

Ochoa worked for Sandia National Laboratories in Livermore, California, and the National Aeronautics and Space Adminstration (NASA) Ames Research Center in California. Her specialty is optical recognition systems, and Dr. Ochoa has presented numerous papers at technical conferences and in scientific journals.

She applied to NASA and became an astronaut in July 1991 when she was thirty-three. By that time, she says, it was generally accepted that women could have any type of career, and 20 percent of the astronaut corps were women. That was a higher percentage of women than she was accustomed to in graduate school or in her earlier jobs.

Ochoa is now a veteran of two space flights. She has logged over 484 hours in space, including a nine-day mission in April 1993.

What difference has being an astronaut made in her life? Not much, according to Ochoa. She took flying lessons but thinks she probably would have done that anyway. And being an astronaut did not keep her from marrying Coe Fulmer Miles of Molalla, Oregon, or from her hobbies of playing the classical flute, volleyball, and bicycling. Now she's added private piloting to that list.

Charmayne James-Rodman

Barrel Racing Champion
1970—

Barrel racing is a standard rodeo event in which three barrels are evenly spaced on the arena floor in a triangular pattern. The horse and rider must circle each barrel, riding around the three in a cloverleaf pattern. The winner is the rider who performs the intricate pattern in the shortest time—eighteen seconds is a good time. Knocking a barrel over means a five-second penalty. Only women participate in the barrel-race event in rodeos sanctioned by the Professional Rodeo Cowboy Association (PRCA). Cowboys joke that they're too smart to take the risk.

Born in Texas and raised in tiny Clayton, New Mexico, Charmayne James rode as soon as she walked and can't remember a time when she didn't ride horseback. By the time she was six years old, she was winning in horse shows and rodeos, and when she was eleven she won enough to pay her own entry fees. "My dad told me I could rodeo if I could pay my way," she once said.

She began barrel racing as an after-school hobby in her early teens with a horse called Scamper. The colt had been banished from the family feedlot for being difficult and liking to buck, but Scamper and Charmayne were an instant team and they hit the rodeo trail. In 1984, when she was an eighth-grader, Charmayne and her mother logged 80,000 miles (129,000 km) traveling to rodeo events approved by the Women's Professional Rodeo Association (WPRA). She was named "Rookie of the Year," the first-year WPRA member who won the most money. At the National Finals Rodeo she clocked the fastest time and won the racing average, thereby earning the title World Champion Barrel Racer and the gold belt buckle that goes with the title. In 1987, she was the first barrel racer to earn more money than any PRCA rodeo cowboy.

By 1992, Charmayne had won nine buckles, was earning more than $100,000 each year, and had been featured in *Sports Illustrated, Seventeen, People Magazine, Grit Weekly Newspaper* and regional and horse publications. She had appeared on television on "ABC Sunday News" and "PM Magazine" and had twice been entered in the *Guinness Book of World Records.* She was inducted into the Panhandle Sports Hall of Fame at Amarillo College, the National Cowgirl Hall of Fame, and the PRCA Hall of Champions.

While keeping up the hectic pace of a rodeo competitor, Charmayne finished high school as an honor student and a member of her school's track and basketball teams. With her early winnings, she bought a pickup, a horse trailer, and rodeo equipment, set aside money for college, and adopted two children through a foreign-relief service. Later, she bought cattle and fed them at her father's feedlot and invested in Ritesuff—her father's line of balanced horse feed, She also developed a barrel-racing saddle that was marketed nationally.

Without Scamper, Charmayne might not have rewritten barrel-racing history. The horse has won his share of honors, too. He was selected for several years as the American Quarter Horse Association's (AQHA) Barrel Horse of the Year and awarded the second Silver Spur ever given by the AQHA. (Cisco, the buckskin ridden by Kevin Costner in *Dances with Wolves* got the first.) Rodeo people call Scamper "Super Horse" and the "Horse with the Most Heart." In December 1985, at the National Finals Rodeo, Charmayne rode Scamper around the barrels without a bridle—and won the round! His headstall had accidentally come off as Charmayne waited for her turn at the barrels. At the first barrel, the horse still had the bit in his mouth, but it dropped off, and Charmayne just held on and rode.

Charmayne James married California team roper Walt Rodman in 1988 and now makes her home in California. And she's still racing and riding . . . .

Shannon Miller

Olympic Gymnast
1977–

Shannon Miller vaulted into international fame during the 1992 Summer Olympics in Barcelona, Spain, when she won five medals—more than any other United States athlete. By the time of the 1996 Olympics in Atlanta, Georgia, she had become America's most decorated gymnast, with eight world championship medals. She was the only U.S. woman to win the all-around world gymnastics championship title two years in a row (1993 and 1994).

But as the 1996 games approached,

there was doubt that Miller could keep up her championship record. She was nineteen years old—young by most standards but, as one reporter put it, "over 100 in gymnast years," in a sport where competitors are often as young as thirteen and fourteen. Since 1992, Miller had grown in both height and weight, changing the center of gravity in her body and, consequently, the way it responded during various exercises. But Shannon Miller is a girl of dogged determination. She has said she went to the 1996 Olympics to show herself she could do it and to show other older gymnasts that they could do it too.

She was born in Missouri in March 1977, but her family moved to Edmond, Oklahoma, when she was six months old. Her father teaches physics at the University of Central Oklahoma and uses videotapes of his daughter's gymnastic routines to illustrate gravity, movement, and force to his classes; her mother is a banking executive. Miller, the second of three children, has an older sister and a younger brother.

When the two girls were preschoolers, their parents bought them a trampoline. Before long, the girls were flipping in the air everywhere—on the trampoline, in the house, and at school. Concerned for their safety, their parents enrolled them in a gymnastics class. Miller's sister attended the classes for a couple of years and then moved on to other interests, but Miller had found something she loved. By the time she was nine, she had made the junior team of the U. S. Association of Independent Gymnastics Clubs.

A two-week training camp in the former Soviet Union in 1986 was a turning point for her, because it made her realize that gymnastics was more than fun. It was hard work. She saw how good the Soviets were at the sport and decided that she wanted to be that good. At the training camp, she was noticed by Steve Nunno, an Oklahoma City coach, with whom she has trained since.

While training six hours a day six days a week, Miller attended public high school in Edmond and graduated with a 3.96 grade point average. Her only B was in a sophomore geometry class. In 1995 when the teacher of that class became ill with cancer, Miller organized a celebrity auction for his benefit and asked for donations from other Olympic athletes. She raised $5,000 for the family of the teacher, just a week before he died.

Although the 1992 Olympics made her a celebrity, Miller took it all in stride. "I still go to public school," she told an interviewer, "and my brother and sister still pick on me, and I pick on them."

During her career, she suffered a series of injuries—a pulled hamstring that kept her from training for two months in 1989 and a pulled stomach muscle and shin splints in 1994. But she came back from each injury, and she has competed even while in pain. Nunno calls her "focused" and when accused of pushing her, says she always pushed herself.

Miller is admittedly shy and introverted, and she seldom smiles while performing. Nor does she look at the audience—she is totally involved in her routine. Like many gymnasts, she's occasionally prone to tears.

Those tears came out in the 1996 Olympics when, after a strong performance on the balance beam she flubbed her floor exercises and walked off the floor crying, knowing that she would not win the gold medal. In the next round, she fell on her second vault and finished last. But the following day, in her final chance at an individual gold medal, Miller turned in a flawless performance on the balance beam and won the gold. It now rests in her trophy cabinet in Oklahoma, along with all the other awards she has won. And Shannon Miller had proved that nineteen is not old—even in gymnastics.

At the close of the 1996 Olympics, Shannon Miller went back to the University of Oklahoma, where she had taken classes while training. She has mentioned the possibility of going into sports medicine and said she hopes to marry and have children someday. Her career as a gymnast might well be over, but Miller's determination and discipline will surely take her in new and highly successful directions.

For Further Information

Biographies and Memoirs

Alderman, Clifford Lindsey. *Annie Oakley and the World of Her Time*. New York: Macmillan, 1979.

Alderson, Nannie T., and Helena Huntington Smith. *A Bride Goes West*. Lincoln: University of Nebraska Press, 1969.

Boutelle, Sara Holmes. *Julia Morgan, Architect*. New York: Abbeville Press, 1988.

Cayleff, Susan E. *Babe. The Life and Legend of Babe Didrikson Zaharias*. Champagne/Urbana: The University of Illinois Press, 1955.

Chaput, Don. *Nellie Cashman and the North American Mining Frontier*. Tucson, Arizona: Westernlore Press, 1995.

Darling, Gail. *Etta Place: Her Life and Times with Butch Cassidy and the Sundance Kid*. Plano, Texas: Republic of Texas Press, 1996.

Fisher, Lillian M. *Brave Bessie, Flying Free*. Dallas: Hendrick-Long, 1995.

Flynn, Jean. *Lady: A Biography of Claudia Alta (Lady Bird) Johnson, Texas' First Lady*. Austin, Texas: Eakin Press, 1992.

Haskins, James. *Barbara Jordan*. New York: Dial Press, 1977.

Kreischer, Elsie Karr. *María Montoya Martínez, Master Potter.* Gretna, Louisiana: Pelican Publishing, 1995.

Rogers, Roy. *Happy Trails: Our Life Story.* New York: Simon & Schuster, 1994.

Sandweiss, Martha A. *Laura Gilpin: An Enduring Grace.* Fort Worth: Amon Carter Museum, 1986.

Stewart, Elinore Pruitt. *Letters of a Woman Homesteader.* Lincoln: University of Nebraska Press, 1961.

Stillwell, Hallie Crawford. *I'll Gather My Geese.* College Station: Texas A&M University Press, 1991.

Tobias, Tobi. *Maria Tallchief.* New York: Crowell, 1970.

Turner, Robyn. *Georgia O'Keeffe.* New York: Little, Brown, 1991.

Venezia, Mike. *Georgia O'Keeffe.* Chicago: Children's Press, 1993.

General Reference

Abernethy, Francis Edward, ed. *Legendary Ladies of Texas.* Denton: University of North Texas Press,

Alter, Judith. *Women of the Old West.* New York: Franklin Watts, 1989.

The Handbook of Texas. Austin: Texas State Historical Association, 1996.

McLeRoy, Sherrie S. *Red River Women.* Plano, Texas: Republic of Texas Press, 1996.

Reiter, Joan Swallo. *The Women.* The Old West Series. Alexandra, Virginia: Time-Life Books, 1978.

Roach, Joyce Gibson. *The Cowgirls.* Denton: University of North Texas Press, 1990.

Robertson, Janet. *The Magnificent Mountain Women: Adventures in the Colorado Rockies.* Lincoln: University of Nebraska Press, 1990.

Schlissel, Lillian, ed. *Women's Diaries of the Westward Journey.* New York: Schocken Books, 1982.

Sinnott, Susan. *Extraordinary Asian Pacific Americans.* Chicago: Children's Press, 1993.

Underwood, Larry. *Love and Glory: Women of the Old West.* Lincoln, Nebraska: Media Publishing, 1991.

Western Writers of America. *The Women Who Made the West.* New York: Doubleday, 1980.

Web Sites of Interest

Susan Butcher:
http://www.iditarod.com/

Willa Cather:
http://icg.fas.harvard.edu/~cather

Bessie Coleman:
http://www.ninety-nines.org/coleman.html
http://www.dotstate.mn.us/aeronautics/bessie.html
http://www.eng.fu.edu/aero/coleman.htm

Edna Gladney:
http://www.netvideo.com/mediamart/video/rel/sku/mmm102202.html

Henriette Wyeth Hurd:
http://www.wic.org/bio/hwyeth.htm

Ladybird Johnson:
http://www.wildflower.org/

María of San Ildefonso:
http://www.viva.com/nm/PCCmirror/sanildef.html

Shannon Miller:
http://www.yahoo.com/Recreation/Sports/Gymnastics/Gymnasts/Miller_Shan

Georgia O'Keeffe:
http://www.ionet.net/~jellenc/Okeeffe2.html
http://www.okeeffe.museum.org

Mari Sandoz:
http://www.csc.edu/library/resources/SANDOZ/SANDOZ2.html

Amy Tan:
http://www.alchemyweb.com/~alchemy/amytan/

Laura Ingalls Wilder
http://webpages.marshall.edu/!irby/laura.htmix

Museums and Archive Collections

The Georgia O'Keeffe Museum
313 Read Street
Santa Fe, New Mexico 87501
505-995-0785

The National Cowgirl Hall of Fame and Western Heritage Center
111 West Fourth Street Suite 300
Fort Worth, Texas 76102
817-336-4475

Women Writing the West
P.O. Box 12
Boulder, Colorado 80306-0012
Web site under development

Index

Numbers in *italics* represent illustrations.

Photo Credits

Photographs ©: American Heritage Center/University of Wyoming: 3, 26, 34, 36; Amon Carter Museum, Forth Worth, TX: 6, 180 (Bequest of Laura Gilpin, 1979); AP/Wide World Photos: 8, 234; Archive Photos: 110 (American Stock), cover right, 7, 210; Arizona Historical Society/Tucson: 4, 6, 27, 74, 172; Austin History Center, Austin Public Library, #E.4 D 20: 6, 158; Brown Brothers: 6, 153; Cheney Cowles Museum/ Eastern Washington State Historical Society, Spokane, Washington: 3, 5, 21, 103; Corbis-Bettmann: 8, 259 (Reuters), 6, 184 (Underwood & Underwood), cover far right, 5, 6, 7, 8, 117, 157, 165, 204, 231, 245, 261 (UPI), 3, 4, 6, 14, 30, 46, 169; Dadie Potter: 7, 196; Dallas Public Library, Texas/Dallas History and Archives Division: 6, 161; Denver Public Library, Western History Department: 5, 92; Gamma-Liaison: 8, 250 (Karl Gehring), 223 (Zigy Kaluzny), 8, 240 (Molina-Bendi), cover center, 8, 254 (James Schnepf), 8, 271; Hearst Newspaper Collection, Special Collections, University of Southern California Library: 7, 189, 200; Kansas Collection, University of Kansas Libraries: 81; Kansas State Historical Society, Topeka: 3, 10; LBJ Library Collection: 225 (Robert Knudsen); Little Bighorn Battlefield National Monument: 5, 97; Montana Historical Society, Helena: 151 (Mackay Collection), 4, 5, 6, 83, 85, 126, 129, 131, 149; Museum of Modern Art: 5, 133 (Photograph by Steichen); Museum of New Mexico: 3, 18; NASA: 266; Nebraska State Historical Society: 5, 7, 99, 135, 192; Nevada State Museum, Carson City, NV: 4, 67; New York Public Library Picture Collection: 4, 79, 89, 90; Oregon Historical Society: 4, 58; Panhandle-Plains Historical Museum: 4, 63; Roy Rogers-Dale Evans Museum: 7, 228; Sisters of Providence Archives, Seattle, WA: 3, 41, 44; Superstock, Inc.: 5, 112 (Christie's Images); Supreme Court Historical Society: 8, 237; Texas State Library & Archives Commission: 4, 6, 51, 52, 142; United States Postal Service: 187 (Stamp Service Archive); Ursuline Convent: 4, 55; Utah State Historical Society: 4, 33, 70 (Photograph Archives), 6, 146; Western History Collections, University of Oklahoma Library: cover left, 5, 6, 29, 109, 122, 137, 176; Western History Research Center, University of Wyoming: 16; Women's Army Corps Museum Fort McClellan, AL: 7, 216; Women's Professional Rodeo Association: 8, 268 (Kenneth Springer).

About the Author

Judy Alter considers herself a woman of the American West by adoption. Born in Illinois, she has lived in Texas for over thirty years and traveled widely in the West. She is the author of nearly thirty books, both fiction and nonfiction, many dealing with women of the West. She has won several awards, including Best Juvenile Novel of 1984 from the Texas Institute of Letters, Best Western Novel from Western Writers of America, and two Western Heritage (Wrangler) Awards from the National Cowboy Hall of Fame.

Asked why she writes so often about women in the West, she explains that the Western environment shaped women's lives in very different ways from their Eastern sisters and gave them new and exciting opportunities. The women in this book accepted the challenges of the American West and triumphed.

Alter is also the author of several nonfiction books for young readers, including *Rodeo: The Best Show on Dirt, The Santa Fe Trail,* and *Women of the Old West* (all published by Grolier).

When she's not writing, Alter is the director of TCU Press in Fort Worth, Texas. The mother of four now-grown children, she presides over a household that includes two large dogs and two cats.